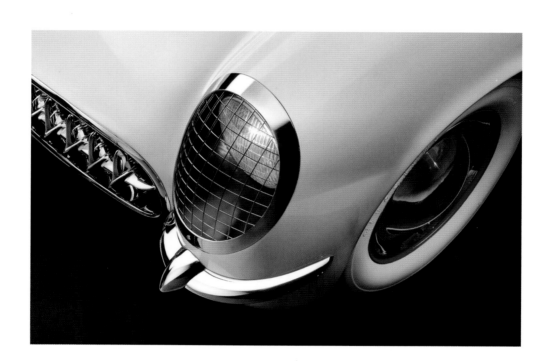

LEGENDARY
Corvettes
'VETTES MADE FAMOUS ON TRACK AND SCREEN

Randy Leffingwell
Photography by Dave Wendt

motorbooks

Dedications:

For John Amgwert, historian, documentarian, researcher, restorer, editor, and friend.
Randy Leffingwell
Santa Barbara, CA

For my brother, Dan Wendt, my best driver.
Dave Wendt
Cinncinati, OH

First published in 2010 by Motorbooks, an imprint of MBI Publishing Company, 400 First Avenue North, Suite 300, Minneapolis, MN 55401 USA

ISBN-13: 978-0-7603-3774-5

Editor: Peter Schletty
Design Manager: Kou Lor
Book and cover design by: John Barnett, 4Eyes Design
Layout by: Chris Fayers

Printed in China

Frontis: Chevrolet's concept of the sports car incorporated headlight stone guards. Earlier cars used 1953 Bel Air wheelcovers because Corvette "Spinner" covers weren't ready by the time production started on June 30, 1953.

Title page: Despite the AAMA recommendation against motorsports promotion, Ed Cole approved a "customer racing package" for the new Sting Ray. This car and three others introduced the package to the racing world at Riverside International Raceway in October 1962.

Cover: Bunkie Knudsen, Ed Cole, and Zora Duntov had planned to assemble 125 of these Grand Sport coupes to take on the best race cars from around the world. Duntov even dreamed of a "production" version of 1,000 copies, but GM's chairman vetoed the project.

Back cover, top left: During the 23rd hour of the 1960 Le Mans race, the engine began seriously overheating. A quick-thinking mechanic packed the engine compartment with ice from the team owner's trailer, and driver Bob Grossman cruised around the track taking 15 minutes for each lap that had required just 5:15 earlier in the race.

Bottom left: Headed for action, George Maharis and Martin Milner leapt from their Tasco Turquoise convertible. For the first season, Chevrolet provided cars in this color, which challenged the cinematographer. Later cars were in Fawn Beige. *The Everett Collection, Inc.*

Top right: Track testing at Waterford Hills outside Detroit led Chevrolet R&D engineers to increase Grand Sport wheel widths from 6 inches to 9 inches on the front and 11 inches on the rear. This took skid pad capability from 0.9g up to 1.1g.

Contents

1953

CORVETTE #003

IN THE BEGINNING, THERE WAS . . .

"Years ago this land knew cars that were fabricated out of sheer excitement," the advertising copywriters wrote. "Magnificent cars that uttered flame and rolling thunder from exhaust pipes as big around as your forearm, and came towering down through the summer dust of American roads like the Day of Judgment."

With words like these, the enthusiasts at Campbell-Ewald were just getting started. Sports car advertising in early 1953 was an unpracticed and untested art in America.

"They were the sports cars," they continued, "in a day when all motoring was an adventure . . .

"They have been ghosts for forty years, but their magic has never died. And so, today, they have an inheritor—for the Chevrolet Corvette reflects, in modern guise, the splendor of their breed."

But for the readers of *True: The Man's Magazine* and other printed target publications, the writers and photographers weren't done. The low, wide, white form streaking off the page left audiences with one last plea for understanding, acceptance, and the birth of desire:

"It is what they were: a vehicle designed for the pure pleasure of road travel. It handles with a precision that cannot be duplicated by larger cars—and it whistles through curves as though it were running on rails."

It was big talk, and it spoke of the brain child of two big men. They were caught in the midst of interesting times. Trying to figure out what the public wanted was not easy.

The story really started in July 1951. The Korean War raged. In Washington, D.C., the federal government tried to determine how much ordnance it should buy without interrupting civil production, as it had done a few years earlier. Soldiers, home from Europe and Asia with unspent paychecks, longed for products denied to them and their families for years. President Harry Truman hoped to not interrupt an economic growth spurt. Yet, to appease the restive work force, he allowed organized labor to strike. The result was chaos. Government agencies responsible for material allocations made questionable decisions, resulting in spot shortages of nickel, copper, and sheet steel. General Motors shut down six plants for a short time in the fall of 1951 as it suffered raw materials shortages. Congress urged auto manufacturers to build smaller cars that conserved materials. However, after a short recession in the middle of 1951 in which some makers sales dropped badly, there was plenty of demand for cars. And ironically, luxury models sold at a premium.

Chevrolet lost a sizable share of the market in 1951. In truth, no maker's cars, not GM, Ford, Packard, or Studebaker, sold as healthily as they had in 1950 except for one company: Chrysler. Plymouth doubled its market share in 1951. Dodge, Chrysler, and De Soto were the only others to increase sales. Chrysler Corporation assessed its chances of climbing up the food chain. To emphasize its ambition, the company launched a small bomb, and when the smoke cleared, it had hit a very big target.

__Chevrolet wrestled with manufacturing__ the sports car with a steel body. However metal stamping dies cost too much and would have taken too long to create for a car management wanted to hurry into the marketplace.

Chevrolet had promised that Corvette production would begin June 30, 1953. Car #001 rolled off the Flint assembly line on time. Body assembler Tony Kleiber (behind the wheel), Flint plant manager F.J. Fessenden (left rear), and Chevrolet assembly plants general manager R.G. Ford beamed like proud parents. At the far left, car #003 prepares for body drop. Courtesy GM Media

Harley Earl wanted a V-8 for the Corvette, but only the Cadillac, Oldsmobile, and Buick divisions had them, and they refused to offer theirs to Chevrolet. Chevrolet engineering chief Ed Cole and his assistant Harry Barr beefed up the 235-cubic-inch displacement inline six using three Carter carburetors and other upgrades to boost output to 150 horsepower. They mated the engine to a two-speed Powerglide automatic transmission.

Chrysler hosted an engineering show. The corporation opened it to the media, and members of the general public snuck in. In the United States, there already were sports cars around—spindly English MG-TC models and lithe, sleek Jaguar XK-120s, along with aristocratic Aston Martins and plebian Triumphs. English-American hybrids from Allard (powered with Cadillac engines) and Nash-Healey shared the roads with all-American creations from race car builder Frank Kurtis and yachtsman/sportsman Briggs Cunningham. But in Chrysler's show, there were new models. One was terrific, a sleek two-seater cloaked in a handsome steel body designed by Ghia in Italy surrounding Chrysler's specially prepared Hemi V-8. This Chrysler's K-310 was striking, and it looked advanced for its day.

Whether Harley Earl, GM's head of Styling Section got in to the show is open to conjecture. Other influences already were assaulting his attention.

While corporate chairman Alfred Sloan may have been the first to deify Earl's skills, it was Buick division general manager Harlow "Red" Curtice who used his talents to save the division nearly killed by the 1930s

Depression. Earl's Buicks became crowd-stoppers in auto shows around the United States in 1936, 1937, and 1938. Earl hitched his own star to Curtice's rising constellation. Curtice was a kindred spirit, whereas Earl was less fond of Nicholas Dreystadt, who ran GM's traditional style-leading Cadillac division. He came to Chevrolet in 1946 and was in line for corporate president until his death in 1948. Once GM's board gave Curtice the job in 1952, Earl could do no wrong. And he had ideas and friends who had more ideas.

One of those friends was U.S. Air Force General Curtis LeMay. LeMay owned an Allard and had been involved in a number of Frank Kurtis' racing activities. In the early 1950s, the Sports Car Club of America (SCCA) was struggling with a safety record that made it unpopular with local communities. LeMay welcomed SCCA events onto his runways. The story goes that after one such race, LeMay asked Earl why none of the American manufacturers produced something "my boys can race around these air fields."

Earl already had produced an impressive two-seater on a Buick platform, his large, luxurious Y-Job. It was a design and engineering show piece filled with

Chevrolet designer and engineer Bob McLean *conceived the sports car from the rear axle forward, setting the passenger compartment far back as was the case with many sports cars at the time. First year cars were only available in Polo White with red interiors and black convertible tops that were stored under the fiberglass cover behind the seats.*

driver- and passenger-comfort innovations that added weight and bulk to its 20-foot length. He maneuvered it through the pits at Watkins Glen, New York, in late 1950, to cheer his friend Briggs Cunningham. Briggs campaigned Cadillac V-8-engined sportsters that he ran at Le Mans months before. He was weeks away from completing his prototype C-1 sports car, and he teased Earl, asking him why GM couldn't build "a proper sports car," something he could race instead of having to build his own. The next year, after Briggs had run four of his 1951 C-2R models at Le Mans, Earl arrived at the Glen in the fall in his 16½-foot-long Buick LeSabre. To Cunningham, this still was not a viable sports car. Briggs forged ahead, completing his first C-3 in 1953 using Chrysler's 310-horsepower hemispherical-head V-8. When his cars competed overseas, they brought attention to America's efforts at sports car production, giving him a steady supply of ammunition with which to chide his friend Harley Earl.

One final element remained to catalyze words into action. Not only were others producing sports cars, but some of them used glass reinforced plastic, GRP, to make the car bodies. By 1940, GM was working with the material, collaborating with Owens-Corning and research chemist Dr. R. Games Slater. Slater had woven fibers of fine glass into a mat that he bonded with polyester resins. Owens marketed this product as Fiberglas, and though it was different from GRP, the two became universally known—and confused—as fiberglass.

The boating industry loved it because users could shape it easily and finished hulls required little maintenance. Bill Tritt, founder of Glasspar boats in southern California, took a call from a friend asking him to fabricate a sports car body for a Jeep. Tritt named it the Boxer. He selected a polyester plastic called Vibrin from U.S. Rubber's Naugatuck division to make his GRP. Naugatuck's sales director, Dr. Earl Ebers, wanted to show their product to Detroit's design and manufacturing decision makers, and he helped Tritt produce four more Boxers by February 1952. Good timing put the Boxer in a *Life* Magazine story called "Plastic Bodies for Autos" just as every auto exec experienced Korean wartime steel shortages. Chevrolet engineering contacted Ebers, who promptly drove one of the Boxers from a trade show directly into GM's styling auditorium.

Corvette #003 *went to GM's Tech Center where it was tagged ES-127 as an "engineering staff" vehicle. For nearly a year, the car endured dozens of tests and eventually Tech Center staff replaced the original chassis with a modified prototype that incorporated changes Chevrolet would include on later production models.*

Ebers and his staff showed design engineers how to cast a fender and duplicate it exactly in fiberglass. Engineers and stylists adapted it to experimental car bodies and dream cars. With it, they replaced conventional plaster-of-Paris-over-wood forms, which they normally finished with hand-hammered steel.

Harley Earl concluded that work done with these new materials represented a significant advance in car design/modeling processes. Fiberglass reduced prototype design time from days to hours. In the Tritt/Ebers Boxer, he saw the automobile he had been thinking about.

Starting in the late 1930s, GM invited influential individuals to preview products and glimpse design concepts. While the weak economy killed shows for 1951 and 1952, GM planned a show series called Motorama for 1953. Touring the United States, Harley's designers featured concepts for each division, including Chevrolet for the first time. The division's new general manager Tom Keating had Harlow Curtice's ear. GM's ailing entry-level model line already had snared Cadillac's chief engineer Ed Cole to turn around staid performance and mediocre reliability.

Earl had dreamt up a package in 1951 utilizing an existing frame and drivetrain surrounded by a stylish two-seat body. He believed it could sell for $1,800, half the price of Jaguar's trend-setting XK-120. He

acquired a Jaguar and set it in the design studio to provide his stylists inspiration and a target. He assigned Bob McLean, a recent California Institute of Technology engineering and industrial design graduate, to create the car. He set Duane "Sparky" Bohnstedt to work styling the body for the project. They wanted Cadillac's or Buick's 188-horsepower V-8, but the upper divisions, including Oldsmobile with its own 165-horsepower engine, jealously guarded their technological advances; it was their marketing advantage. So McLean had Chevy's redoubtable inline 115-horsepower six, penciling it into his package drawings. Like the Jaguar and other sports cars, long hoods and short rear decks were part of the tradition, so McLean began with the same 102-inch wheelbase as the Jaguar and started his design work at the rear axle. He drew in the passenger compartment and drivetrain as he worked forward to the headlights and grille. Because GM advertising language described its cars as "longer, lower, and wider," Bob set front and rear track at 57 and 59 inches respectively, which meant they were 6 and 9 inches greater than the Jaguar. Ed Cole drafted another Cadillac colleague, engine specialist Harry Barr, to tweak the Blue Flame Six with mechanical valve lifters, a new aluminum intake manifold with three Carter carburetors, and a dual exhaust system. This produced a more sporting 150 horsepower.

Maurice Olley's clever chassis provided the car with admirable handling yet was strong enough to handle a decade of power and transmission upgrades. Engine exhaust tips set inboard of the Corvette's tailfins caused problems.

To keep a secret inside a corporation thriving on knowing others' secrets, Earl code-named the project "Opel," and insiders presumed it was an economy two-seater for GM's German partner. Bohnstedt and McLean produced a full-scale clay model that Earl showed to Red Curtice in late spring 1952. Curtice saw it again in June and brought Chevy manager Tom Keating and chief engineer Ed Cole to see it. Every account said Keating and Cole loved it. Some stories say Cole literally jumped up and down. It went to Motorama as Chevrolet's "concept" sports car. They showed it off.

But would they produce it?

That still wasn't a done deal. That required a designer that Harley Earl himself had fired, and a company that was an archrival.

Frank Hershey worked for GM; he had achieved the lofty position of chief of design at Cadillac before Earl fired him for running an outside business making, of all things, ashtrays. Rules in those days were inflexible. Unlike Earl, Hershey didn't much care for sports cars until a GM stylist friend arrived for dinner at his home and pulled out a snapshot of the clay Opel.

Overnight, Hershey was transformed. He bought an XK-120; stole a talented stylist, Bill Boyer, from GM; and assembled a small team of talented designers and engineers to create Ford's answer to GM's sports car. It, too, was based on the Jaguar. In mid-January 1953,

he showed a steel-bodied concept to a small crowd of key people at Ford, just as GM opened the doors on Motorama in New York City. Ford himself loved it and approved it on the spot.

Over the next five months, GM showed the Corvette—named after an aggressive naval warship—to more than a million potential buyers while the show crossed the country. Some 300,000 visitors trouped through the New York Motorama launch in mid-January 1953. GM personnel heard them comment on the Corvette.

"It's lovely."

"It's cute."

"I wish I had one now!"

Keating authorized production to start mid-June as a 1953 model. He and Cole agreed to produce the car in fiberglass. It saved time and money and capitalized on its distinctive novelty. They also decided to switch to steel for 1954 if the public liked it.

With Chevrolet budgets strained, he knew approving series manufacture in fiberglass was prudent because steel dies would have cost five times as much as the master fiberglass forms. Engineers selected Molded Fiber Glass Company in Ashtabula, Ohio, to form the body panels, creating a "recipe" for the composite material that is little changed today.

Corvette assembly at the Flint, Michigan, plant was essentially prototype assembly. They built cars the way old-world craftsmen in Europe produced each example individually by hand. Variation arrived in each car as the process evolved before their eyes.

GM and Chevy divisions were proud of the new car and its unique boxed girder with central X-reinforced frame and fiberglass body material. The company's vast public relations machine chugged out a slow, steady production of stories and photographs of nearly every stage of the process. Most of the early pictures include or illustrate the car that is the subject of this chapter, serial number 3, now the oldest-known surviving 1953 Corvette. The initial handful of cars (some say six of the first nine assembled at the former Customer Delivery Garage at Atherton Road and Van Slyke Avenue in Flint) remained property of General Motors. Three stayed with Chevrolet division for Proving Ground engineering staff at Milford, Michigan. These received additional identifying codes that began with "3" for the model year, "95" for Corvette, and a sequence number. For these cars, #3950 was the first, #3951 was the second, and #3952 was the third.

Three others went to GM's Tech Center in Warren, Michigan. Engineers there identified the cars as Engineering Staff vehicles using a prefix "ES." They already had other cars under tests for many years, so they started with #127 (later changed to 127-1.) Engineers took two more cars, chassis #008 and #009, but which one was ES-128-2 and which was ES-129-3 remains unclear. Coding was for internal record keeping and work tracking. The numbers probably appeared on each car's windshield for easy identification. Each fell under direct supervision of G. C. Kuiper of the engineering-staff passenger-car development garage at the Warren Tech Center.

Flint assembly completed Corvette #001, Proving Grounds #3950, on June 30, 1953. This is the car that appears nearest the camera in all the production line photos of early Corvettes. Harlow Curtice had promised to news media that Chevrolet would produce the first Corvettes in June, and Chevrolet assemblers hurriedly finished #001 and #002 in the last day of the month.

Chevrolet's assistant chief engineer under Ed Cole was Harry Barr. Barr drove #001 to the Proving Ground, where it ran a 1,000-mile break-in. Ed Cole drove it 500 miles farther over the weekend of July 16–17. It rotated

through the engineering staff, and each member added his comments and recommendations to the car's log.

By late July, #3950 required "various revisions to make it a satisfactory production vehicle," and a work order issued August 6 addressed those changes and updates. They rebuilt the folding top, installed new seats, replaced the door locks and fuel filler door, adjusted the side windows to fit the windshield, added reinforcement under the instrument panel for the inside rearview mirror and the steering wheel, added an outside rearview mirror for better visibility when the top was raised, and improved cowl vent controls.

By December 1953, engineering staff reassigned #3950, Corvette #001, to Harley Earl's Styling Section. Whether it became another show car or a future styling proposal is subject to conjecture. But eventually it left GM.

Car #3951, production #002, also went to Milford's Proving Grounds. On July 9, Chevrolet engineer and Indianapolis race winner Mauri Rose evaluated the car and found 22 "deficiencies." These paralleled what Harry Barr, Ed Cole, and other engineers had discovered, which had led to the work order updating all the engineering cars to meet current production standards. On October 26, *another* work order sent #3951 back to the shops "to install a V-8 engine in a 1953 Corvette for mock-up purposes in order to [discover any potential] design problems [that might be] encountered in a 1955 Corvette."

After engineers installed a non-running mockup of the engine, they placed notes on the dashboards and the inner fenders, noting areas that needed modification to fit the larger engine. These moved the battery and shifted the steering column outward to clear exhaust manifolds.

By mid-1954, #3951 with its installed V-8 had completed wind-tunnel cooling tests at Harrison Radiator's laboratory in New York. To accommodate the V-8, engineers replaced the entire frame and suspension and gave it a new fuel system and tank, a new 12-volt electrical system, and a new exhaust system. Then they installed electric windshield wipers and a new fresh-air heater system. Engineers rebuilt the car once more to evaluate ride and put a new body on the chassis in May 1955. They replaced the engine and transmission in August and then drove it through a

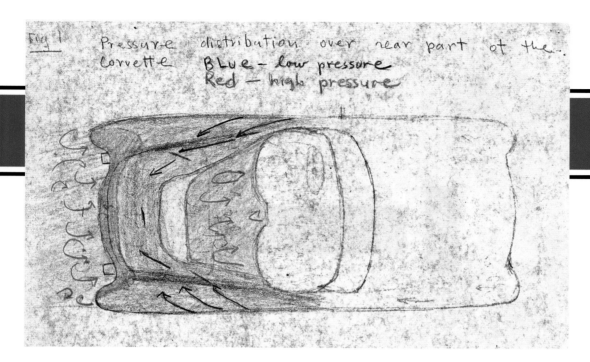

In the image (handwritten notes): *Fig 1* Pressure distribution over rear part of the Corvette. BLue – low pressure. Red – high pressure.

In December 1953, recently hired engineer Zora Arkus-Duntov tackled the issue of engine exhaust staining the paint and seeping into the passenger compartment. This is Zora's original hand-colored drawing showing air flow at speed. His short-term solution changed the exhaust tip design for 1954–55 and relocated tailpipe outlets to the rear corners of the body for 1956. John Amgwert collection

25,000-mile durability test. Russ Sanders, director of the Experimental Department, had the car rebuilt yet again for use as a "courtesy car" for executives and automotive journalists in late 1955. At that point, the car had been transformed from a Polo White inline six to a Gypsy Red V-8, coded-named EX-122. In mid-April 1956, Sanders bought the car for himself.

Corvette #003, the subject of this chapter, went to the Tech Center, where they christened it ES-127. Today, this one has no vehicle identification numbers stamped in the frame, which is unusual for a production car. According to John Amgwert, this car has its fuel and brake lines mounted and running on the inboard side of the right-hand frame rail, as all 1954 models did. The regular production run of 1953 cars had their brake and fuel lines outside the rails. "The modification of the fuel and brake lines is clearly a neat and professional job done by hand," he explained, "and it could not have been done with the body on the chassis."

Amgwert would know this. He was one of the seven founders of the National Corvette Restorers Society (NCRS) in 1974. He also edited their magazine for 25 years and was a partner in owning #003 for 18 years.

"It is our speculation," Amgwert went on, "based on the many details that we've inspected, studied, and compared with numerous other 1953 Corvettes, that the frame with our car was a GM 'mule,' an experimental frame used for testing and fitting both modified front spring gussets and the relocated fuel and brake lines on a vehicle chassis. And that this frame was installed by GM prior to the car being shipped to a retail customer." The rest of the car, including the frame, in Amgwert's experienced judgment, was correct as a very early 1953 production model. The hand-laid fiberglass mounted on the one-piece underbody was consistent with its origin as one of the earliest produced.

Which begs the question: What happened to the original #003 frame? After decades of searching, it turned up under a 1954 six-cylinder body that bore a 1955 V-8 serial number! It appeared to Amgwert "to have been a compilation of parts from several cars. . . . It is our speculation that the original frame stamped zero-zero-three was removed from our car by the Chevrolet Engineering Department in 1953. And that this frame was also used for testing at GM; eventually it went out the backdoor and into private hands—possibly to a GM employee? We believe that parts from several cars may have been put together by one of its owners to make 1955 Corvette number thirteen-twelve."

Chevrolet general manager Thomas Keating planned a cautious launch of Harley Earl's dream sports car. Keating set a first year production target of 300 automobiles, hoping to create a sense of exclusivity. By model year end, though, Chevrolet had delivered just 183.

Harley Earl had hoped the Corvette would debut with a price around $1,800, to compete with modest Triumph and MG models from England. Instead, it arrived at $3,498, very close to his target Jaguar XK-120. Challenges of working with fiberglass yielded cars with poorly fitting body panels, which hurt the car's reputation.

ES-127-1's history was documented from the start, appearing first as Project #360-1-60 on July 7, 1953. The car had just 67 miles on the odometer when a preliminary inspection revealed that its "engine hood panel has become warped, its fiberglass cloth weave is apparent through the white paint, the paint [has] discolored around the fuel filler cap access door, exhaust gas at the rear tail pipe causes permanent discoloration of body paint, and both right and left doors do not close properly." With its failings so noted, G. C. Kuiper and C. H. Jensen climbed in the

car and drove it to Lockport, New York, for the "Cold Room Shake Test."

After a 300-mile drive, Kuiper supervised tests on July 8 and 9 in Harrison Radiator's cold room at -20 degrees Fahrenheit, "to determine low temperature strength characteristics of [the] plastic body." Engineers attached four 3-ounce weights to the front wheel rims, two on each side, at about a 90-degree separation. After leaving the car to chill for two hours in the cold room, engineers ran dynamometers under the front tires at a variety of speeds for five hours at -20 degrees

and could not be pulled shut with the existing door-pull apparatus. The passenger compartment lids on each door flipped open when the doors were slammed, the steering column was not rigidly attached at the instrument panel nor was it centrally located through the hole, and the engine began smoking during the break-in period.

Engineers returned to work, disconnected the driveshaft, and put the unbalanced wheels on the rear. Another two hours to cool the car preceded the next five-hour dyno run as the tires spun through the same range of speeds. No new fractures appeared, but "during the return trip to Detroit, it was apparent that body shake had increased." They also observed that new door latches fitted before they left New York were better but not satisfactory. They also found it difficult to keep the three carburetors synchronized (to such an extent that Chevrolet engineers began immediately to redesign the linkage.) The good news? The engine smoke during break-in had disappeared.

Following another careful inspection, they turned the car over to Charles Chayne, the head of the GM engineering staff, for his use. He put 105 miles on the car, and it went to the Proving Ground for a tune-up and a series of updates. Doors latches still remained a problem, and newly installed side windows produced extreme vibration when the car was driven on rough surfaces. Within days, new door seals, latches, and door striker plates fitted to ES-127-1 remedied the door latch problems. As if that were not enough testing, the car went from there to the Belgian Blocks. This course simulated rough cobblestone roads found around the world. ES-127-1 completed 5,000 miles on the course.

While ES-127-1 was shaking itself on the Belgian Blocks, engineers completed a series of "fixes" for the regular production series. These counted some 22 separate items and included the new door seals, latches, gas tank filler door, and window brackets to hold and secure the side windows; a rebuilt folding top; and a reconfiguration of its fiberglass cover panel, among other things. They quickly applied these updates to their other Engineering Staff cars. A few days later, after discovering that the windshield washer reservoir was mounted high enough in the engine compartment to cause a siphoning effect, engineers put in a work

The engineers observed that the maximum shake came at 33 miles per hour, severe enough for them to observe "twisting across the vehicle." After thoroughly inspecting the car, they found four slight fractures in the fiberglass body and more than two dozen other issues. These ranged from the difficulty of raising and lowering the folding top, to the license plate window fogging because of cold condensation and water entering or condensing and pooling in the trunk. The door seal pressure was so high that the doors did not stay latched while driving on moderately rough roads order lowering the reservoir. On production cars, holes were patched, while on the ES vehicles, all of which were deemed works-in-progress, those holes remain.

Chevrolet Engineering Department Work Order #19013-27 from August 20, 1953, titled "Recondition Technical Center Corvette," made "the various fixes which have been found necessary on regular production cars.

"This [work order] will also cover the Chassis work required. Technical center will replace the Frame and Steering mechanism; therefore, no work is to be done on those items." A day later, a supplemental order was more specific:

"Chevrolet [Engineering] will do only the work that can be done without removing the Body.

"The Technical Center will install a new Frame and other parts in the above list when the Car is returned to them."

The "new frame" was the structure without a VIN number but with relocated brake fluid and fuel lines.

Why was this done? A work order, #19025-2 on July 22, explained: "To eliminate very close clearance condition between Right Rear Spring and Brake Pipe to Rear Brake Hose." After hurried efforts to design and test these and other changes, and to create and install an entire modified chassis under body #003 by late August 1953, production was far enough along that engineering management chose not to recall the early cars. Instead, Chevrolet decided to delay introduction of this frame until the 1954 model cars.

Car 127-1 continued to see engineering and evaluation use at least through October 1953. Sometime late in 1953 or early 1954, Chevrolet delivered the car to California to an as-yet unidentified buyer. A subsequent owner put the car in storage in 1963, where it remained until 1987, when Amgwert, Les Bieri, and Howard Kirsch acquired it.

The next three production cars—#004, #005, and #006—all went to retail customers. Car #004 went to J. Spencer Weed, head of the Grand Union grocery company of New Jersey. A buyer listed as "F. C. Greenwalt" (probably Crawford H. Greenewalt) purchased #005 from Frank Diver, Inc., in Wilmington, Delaware, as well as #006 to Henry B. DuPont. The two latter men were executives in the DuPont Company,

an organization with long-standing ties to GM and its financing. It was Chevrolet's and General Motors' intention to get the few first-year cars into the hands of influential business people as well as entertainment and athletic celebrities.

Car #007 went to the Milford Proving Grounds as #3953 in late July 1953. Over the course of its life at Milford, engineers relocated the carburetor choke and windshield wiper controls so that starting the car would be easier for the driver. In September, engineers replaced its front springs with experimental versions to raise front ride height. When engineers had driven #003, ES-127, out to New York for cold testing, they observed—and noted—that exhaust fumes discolored the back end of the car. Car #3953 was the first vehicle to test lengthened tailpipes and tailpipe extensions to alleviate that problem. In early 1954, car #3953 got a new folding top of Orlon and a new DuPont synthetic, as well as door locks from Chevrolet's Truck Division. Sometime in mid-1954, the car disappeared through Creative Industries, an outside contractor that GM used for custom design work. Its location today is unknown.

Cars #008 and #009 went to the Warren Tech Center, where they joined #003 as ES-128 and ES-129, though no one today knows which was which. As test and evaluation vehicles, the cars received new front and rear shock absorbers (as did car #003) in October 1953. Sometime in 1959, a design center prototype engineer named Waino Husko acquired #008. He used it as his daily driver for a number of years. It got hit several times, and he eventually painted it red before finally parking it in a barn in Romeo, Michigan, in 1970. The car recently sold at auction to Detroit-area Chevrolet dealer Fred Rinke. The whereabouts of #009 is still unknown.

The early Corvettes were not without faults. Some were accidental, but some seemed, in retrospect, to have been calculated. When GM's board approved production as a 1953 model, fiberglass was the only material that could work in time. Chevrolet division set a modest first-year production target of just 300 cars. It hoped to create an exclusive, desirable model that prominent politicians, entertainers, and sports personalities would want. Chevrolet division supervised distribution rather than carefully parceling the few first year cars out to anxious buyers who really wanted the car.

Maurice Olley's chassis, *Bob McLean's engineering, and "Sparky" Bohnstedt's body delivered a car that provided buyers a low, wide stance. The rear-wheel track was 59 inches, 9 inches wider than the Jaguar. It contributed to the car's good handling and comfortable ride.*

With so many new features on the car, GM was justifiably wary of releasing its experiments to the public. It did anticipate more tolerance of potential flaws from upper echelon buyers. But frantic testing and post-introduction development work from Milford and Warren engineering staffs delayed getting cars into the hands of hungry journalists. Journalists got no unproven cars. But the Corvette had been out for several months by September 29, when the first magazines got test vehicles. Its unexceptional Blue Flame Six coupled to a two-speed automatic transmission set journalists' and enthusiasts' teeth on edge. A perceived snobbery on Chevrolet's part put otherwise anxious "civilians" off the car. (The car arrived at dealers priced in Cadillac territory at $3,847 with mandatory radio and heater options.) In 1954, with assembly established at St. Louis and production goals set at 10,000 cars, the end of Corvette's second year saw 1,064 copies unsold out of total manufacturing totals of just 3,640 cars. But the rest is history.

As for #001, rumors still abound. Bill France was a special friend of Chevrolet. He was a celebrity in a number of circles, and he was busy promoting a new series called Sports Cars on Dirt. There are still a few racers around today who remember seeing a very early Corvette on dirt tracks in the southeast in late 1955 and early 1956 racing against Dodges and Fords and Studebakers, and Chevrolet and Pontiac sedans.

It is the stuff of legend and myth. It gets car researchers and detectives squinting far into the distance. But the truth and the fact is that #003 exists, restored by John Amgwert and his partners as it was when it left GM engineering several months after its manufacture. Dave Ressler, a long-time second-generation Chevrolet dealer in Montana and North Dakota, has built a collection of significant models. It includes many "firsts," and this one, which also is the oldest Corvette.

1956

CORVETTE SR SEBRING RACER

THE REAL MCCOY

If Chevrolet's general manager, Tom Keating, was disappointed with Corvette's sales in 1953, he was devastated by what followed in 1954. A ready and willing work force in St. Louis geared up to manufacture and assemble as many as 10,000 cars a year, a huge jump from the 50 or so each month the Flint plant could manage. GM hoped the number might reach 20,000. Marketing efforts perked up the car with new colors to supplement 1953's Polo White. Buyers in 1954 could choose also Sportsman Red, Pennant Blue, and black. Factory bulletins even listed two metallic colors, green and bronze, although St. Louis produced no cars in these colors.

But nothing—not even maneuvering price stickers to make last year's "standard" Powerglide transmission a "mandatory option" at $178.35 in an effort to drop the price of the car—could energize the sluggish momentum that held back sales. Efforts to put the cars into "the right hands" had backfired. Wealthy influential opinion-makers didn't think much of poor fits-and-finish work on the fiberglass body, crude and leaky tops that challenged owners to erect or take down, and other evidence that hinted Chevrolet had rushed a vehicle into production and was relying on buyers to do the final testing. Among another group of wealthy influential opinion-makers— members of GM's board of directors—the car began to look like a failure with little chance of redemption.

Then Ford Motor Company intervened. It announced a two-seater, the Thunderbird, for introduction in the

1955 model year. Keating and GM management refused to halt Corvette production and admit defeat in the face of new competition. The T-bird ensured Corvette's survival. How to make it thrive was another question. That required something only a few wealthy, influential opinion-makers knew much about. It took racing to change the perception of the Corvette as a sports car.

Chevrolet engineer Paul Van Valkenburgh, in his insider history of Chevrolet's backdoor racing programs, *Chevrolet = Racing . . . ? Fourteen Years of Raucous Silence*, summed up the situation. As an engineer working in R&D, he was involved in most of the racing and high-performance programs Chevrolet undertook in the early and mid-1960s. He explained corporate philosophy and its reality: "Chevrolet wasn't building race cars," he wrote, "they were building production sedans that were suitable for racing . . . with the proper optional heavy-duty parts." Cole, as chief engineer of Chevrolet, had encouraged project engineer Harry Barr (who had led development of Cadillac's new V-8) to complete Chevrolet's V-8 engine. This was a simple, functional engine that became, as Van Valkenburgh characterized it, "a benchmark in reciprocating engines." Barr had help from production engineer E. H. Kelley, who concentrated on costs.

Money was important to the division. Using fewer raw materials saved money and weight, another important consideration to racers. The engine's most significant innovation resulted from Barr's decision to

If Duane Bohnstedt's 1953 body styling was the prototype, Bob Caderet's 1956 Corvette was the working model. Relieved of the small front bumpers and the toothy grille, and fitted with driving lights and extra marker lights, the car was a handsome racer.

THE REAL McCOY

Here is the most remarkable car made in America today — the new Chevrolet Corvette.
Why remarkable?
Because it is *two* cars wrapped up in one sleek skin. One is a luxury car with glove-soft upholstery, wind-up windows, a removable hardtop (with virtually 360° vision), or fabric top, ample luggage space, a velvety ride and all the power assists you could want, including power-operated fabric top* and Powerglide transmission*.
The other is a sports car. And we mean the real McCoy, a tough, road-gripping torpedo-on-wheels with the stamina to last through the brutal 12 hours of Sebring, a close-ratio trans-

mission (2.2 low gear, 1.31 second) matched to engine torque characteristics, razor-sharp steering (16 to 1) that puts *command* into your fingertips.
Other people make a luxury car that has much the same dimensions as this. That's not so tough. And the Europeans make some real rugged competition sports cars—and that's considerably tougher. But nobody but Chevrolet makes a luxury car that *also* is a genuine 100-proof sports car.
It's a wicked combination to work out, and we didn't hit it overnight. But you'll find, when you take the wheel of a new Corvette, that the result is fantastic—the most heart-lifting blend of all the things you've ever wanted a car to be.

If you find it hard to believe that one car could combine such widely different characteristics we can't blame you. And no amount of talk can tell you half so much as 15 minutes in a Corvette's cockpit—so why don't you let your Chevrolet dealer set up a road test of the most remarkable car made in America today? . . . Chevrolet Division of General Motors, Detroit 2, Michigan.

*Powerglide and power-operated fabric top optional at extra cost.

CORVETTE

eliminate the common rocker arm shaft. Each stamped rocker arm pivoted around a ball on its own stud. This simpler configuration eliminated other hardware and weight, permitting the engine to reach higher speeds. Barr designed an engine with a short piston stroke good for 5,600 rpm, and Cole had engineers test it for 36 hours at 5,500 rpm just to be sure. The 265-cubic-inch displacement engine developed 162 horsepower. Substituting a four-barrel carburetor for the standard two-barrel and fitting dual exhausts increased output to 180. But as Van Valkenburgh wrote, it was "hardly a *racing* engine."

Except it was. Smokey Yunick got his hands on a couple of the new 1955 Chevy V-8s and soon the cars were winning on the short courses in NASCAR. Chevy's ad agency Campbell-Ewald pushed its copywriters into overdrive and they pumped out ads in national magazines and local papers. The agency convinced Ed Cole to contribute an engineering series to *Popular Mechanics* magazine. Where Chryslers won on the big ovals, smaller lighter Chevys ran farther on softer tires on short tracks and won time after time. By late 1955, Ford, which had seen sales of its T-bird take off beyond all expectations, was aware of the effect Chevrolet's NASCAR victories had on its image as bestselling car in America. While Ford helped privateers field entries in NASCAR, it pushed the Thunderbird into speed trials head-to-head against the Corvette along Daytona Beach.

Zora Arkus-Duntov, a Russian émigré born in Belgium, had studied engineering in Germany. Having seen the Corvette at the Motorama display in New York, he wrote a letter to Cole outlining his thoughts about the car and his ambition to work for Chevrolet. Cole

hired him into Chevrolet engineering in May 1953, a month before production began. It was too late for Duntov to work on the first production models, but it was the car that brought him to Chevrolet. He put all his effort and passion into improving it. Within months he made his opinions known, most famously with a memo to Cole proposing that Chevrolet produce engine parts and chassis performance upgrades to sell to the public so owners could turn Chevy's cars—specifically the Corvette—into the car the customers wanted it to be.

Some of Duntov's challenges originated from Maurice Olley's decision to save time and money by modifying a sedan chassis to use underneath the Corvette. Choices Olley had made to render the car's handling "safe" initially made it less predictable at racing speeds. (The chassis, of course, went on to serve the Corvette well—in racers and on the streets— through the 1962 model year.) Duntov felt the three-speed manual transmission was an improvement over the two-speed automatic but he believed its ratios were

Chevrolet had to retain "production car" status for its racers entered at Sebring. Engineers Andy Rosenberg and Russ Sanders hurried all the modifications Fitch and company developed at Sebring into production at the St. Louis factory.

too widely spread. Its non-synchronized first gear led him to push for a four-speed gearbox. The car's brakes were his biggest challenge. With feedback from successful amateur competitors John Fitch and Dr. Dick Thompson, Duntov convinced management to authorize development and then to introduce specially-finned brake drums with semi-metallic linings, steering arm adapters to quicken steering response, and heavy-duty front and rear springs and anti-sway bars to stabilize handling. It was the force of Duntov's personality that became his biggest challenge; he irked and annoyed colleagues and management alike to get what he felt was best for the sports car he adopted as his own.

Chevrolet had set records racing up Pikes Peak in Colorado in several of its sedans in 1955, with Duntov behind the wheel of one of the fastest cars. For 1956, Ford showed up to challenge the performance and Chevrolets (though without Duntov, who had gotten hurt in a testing accident at GM's proving grounds in Milford, Michigan) again set best times climbing the mountain.

Following Pikes Peak, Cole and Duntov strategized ways to bring the Corvette into action. Each year NASCAR founder Bill France hosted Speed Week along Daytona Beach. Cole and Duntov hatched the plan to take a number of cars to the beach and for at least one of them to hit 150 miles per hour. GM president Tom Keating, following chairman Alfred Sloan's advice to give products time to find their market, approved Corvette production for two additional years through 1957. By the time he did this, however, management once again had left Chevrolet division with little time to make substantial changes.

GM designers tasked with Corvette styling had been thrilled by Cisitalias and Jaguars in the early 1950s. By 1954, they took inspiration from Mercedes-Benz designer Paul Bracq and his 300 SL with its vertical headlights and two gentle engine clearance bulges in the hood. Clare MacKichan and stylist Bob Caderet sculpted taillights into the Corvette's 1956 bodywork and they introduced a long scalloped cove into the body side. Engineering provided roll-up windows with optional power lifts. The new cloth top also offered power lift. (Keating approved all these changes in February 1955; this was so late in the production process that if Corvettes had been manufactured in steel bodies, the 1956 car would have appeared in time for the *1957* model year.)

Chevy chief engineer **Ed Cole** committed two of his engineering staff development cars as well as a third pre-production model to Sebring. He assigned staff engineer Frank Burrell to assist John Fitch in turning the 1956 production car into a Sebring racer.

Chevrolet engineers worked on the 265-cubic inch V-8. They fitted two Carter four-barrel carburetors. They bored out this engine to 307 cubic inches and added a German

Engineers tweaked the 265-cubic-inch V-8 to achieve 210 horsepower for the Corvette with a single Carter WCFB four-barrel carburetor. A second four-barrel boosted output to 225. Duntov's camshaft, developed at the Arizona test track in late 1955, coupled with the dual-four-barrel carburetor intake produced 240 horsepower. But it was speed and performance measured against competitors that registered on American car buyers. Jaguar's XK-120, in hottest trim, reached 130 miles per hour. The Mercedes-Benz 300SL hit 146. To Duntov and Cole, it was essential the Corvette beat that figure. Duntov believed he needed another 30 horsepower, and he had a new camshaft in mind to find that power. Cole sent Duntov back to GM's Phoenix test track to begin to accomplish that goal. But that was just one part of the longer-term and much bigger plan.

Endurance races in Europe brought sports car manufacturers prestige and sales no advertising budget could deliver. Cole wondered if entering Corvettes in America's only internationally sanctioned race—the 12 Hours of Sebring in March 1956—could bring a similar cachet to his sports car.

Besides Duntov, Cole had three-time Indianapolis 500 race winner Mauri Rose on his engineering staff. Rose served as liaison between Chevrolet and the NASCAR racing efforts. In mid-December, while Duntov was in Arizona, Cole brought in Rose, engine wizards Harry Barr and Walter Mackenzie, engine and transmission trouble shooter Maurice "Rosey" Rosenberger, chief of passenger car design Russell Sanders, and two outsiders, Briggs Cunningham, and Cunningham's lead driver John Fitch. Fitch already had finished first, second, or third in dozens of races for Briggs, for Mercedes-Benz, and, earlier, in cars he had built himself. Cole asked Fitch to head the effort to make the Corvette—a car that began as a boulevard cruiser with no racing lineage—into a durable racer that could match or better the performance, reliability, and heritage of the best Europe could offer.

Down in Daytona, December slipped into January before Duntov got his best run. He met his goal—averaging 150.58 miles per hour in both directions using a 240-horsepower engine modified with his camshaft, among other parts Duntov hoped to make available for over-the-counter sales.

At the same time, Cole and engineer Frank Burrell learned that the Fédération International de l'Automobile (FIA), which sanctioned the 12-hour race at Sebring, required that modifications to automobiles entered in production classes had to be available to consumers. Furthermore, rules required manufactures to assemble 25 identical models of a car for it to be considered "production." Chevrolet created a new model, the "SR," which first appeared in a memo from Russ Sanders on January 6, 1956.

Fitch got to Sebring on February 18. After a quick detour to Daytona for the Speed Week events (and his own run at 145.543 miles per hour,) he quickly sized up the problems he saw with the car. "From the very outset of our preparation for Sebring," he told interviewer Richard Prince, "two things were apparent. Corvettes, as they were being delivered from the factory for all-around touring were not, however, equipped or prepared for the specialized rigors of a big-league endurance race—and we had practically no time in which to make them so." Race day was March 24, five weeks away. What compounded his challenge was that he had none of the potential race cars to work on. All Chevrolet could spare him was Zora's tired Arizona proving-ground mule, "a cobbled together 1955 body over a 1956 chassis, with a few experiments in between," he explained.

Fitch determined that Chevy needed to adjust gear ratios in the three-speed transmission if no GM- or outside-manufactured four-speed was available. He questioned the car's over-steering tendencies, and he and Cunningham worried aloud about the light steering and the steering wheel placement too near the driver's chest. He suggested revising the suspension; hard braking dipped the nose, making the headlights nearly useless for night racing. He recommended doubling fuel capacity to run farther between pit stops.

In the course of days of hard driving, Fitch's "mule" leaked oil, threw fan belts, overheated, blew rear ends, broke steering and suspension pieces, destroyed its brakes, and loosened motor mounts. He, Mauri Rose, and Walter Mackenzie worked nearly around the clock with their mechanics to improve the cars. "It was quite some time," Fitch told Prince, "before we could finish a full lap at racing speed before something let go."

Sebring is a tough track. Its cracked concrete surface and 5.2-mile lap length had defeated many well-developed cars for decades.

Cole committed his two 1956 engineering development cars plus a third pre-production model to the Sebring race. He purchased a four-speed German ZF transmission for evaluation. He assigned Frank Burrell, a staff engineer from Cadillac, to run this new project; Burrell had come to Chevrolet with Cole after helping Cunningham's Cadillac coupes at Le Mans. After the Daytona runs, Cole moved Duntov's record car to Sebring as Fitch's fourth racer, converted from speed runs to road racing. Even after these cars arrived, Fitch continued development work only with the mule. Then he adapted changes and upgrades to the racers. To retain "production car" classification for three of the cars, Chevrolet engineers Andy Rosenberg and Russ Sanders hurried into production at the St. Louis plant all the modifications developed at Sebring.

Engineering equipped Fitch's three production and single "prototype" models with the camshaft Duntov had developed to propel his car on Daytona Beach, as well as a 37-gallon gas tank, seat belts, heavy-duty clutch, and Halibrand lightweight magnesium quick change wheels. Halibrand wasn't ready with the disc brakes it was developing, so Fitch and Burrell settled for Chevrolet's newly developed brakes with wider shoes, the so-called Big Brakes. The production cars ran with stock Borg-Warner three-speed transmissions coupled to 265-cubic-inch V-8 engines with dual carburetors and Duntov's special cam. Fitch had one car fitted with a 4.11:1 final drive and established a 6,000 rpm redline with the driver instructed to use all three gears and the full engine range. The second and third production car ran taller final drive gears and he told their drivers to use second and third gear to lessen transmission wear. The "prototype" ran a V-8 engine bored out to 307 cubic inches. This incorporated the Duntov cam and the same dual four-barrel intake system. They mounted the four-speed ZF transmission on it. The displacement increase transferred the car to B/Modified class while the others remained in C production. Fitch "hoped this car, co-driven by Walt Hansgen, would make a show of speed and give the Corvette's many supporters something to cheer about."

Sixty cars started the race. Two "production" Corvettes quit early; car No. 5 retired with a broken rear axle after an hour, and an hour later No. 7 went out with a burnt piston. The third production entry, No. 15, lost first and second gears in the first hour and had to negotiate the entire circuit using only third gear for the remaining 11 hours. The engine's massive torque accelerated the car out of the corners. It finished fifteenth overall. John Fitch's B-class car No. 1 gave him nervous moments when its clutch started slipping on the second lap. But his years of Le Mans experience with Cunningham had taught him to nurse cars and he understood the importance of doing that now.

"I knew that failure at Sebring," he explained to Prince, "would probably mean the end of Chevrolet's interest in racing sports cars. This would be a sad conclusion to all our efforts."

He and co-driver Walt Hansgen finished ninth overall, first in Class B. Chevrolet won the official team prize and the Corvette team won the official production sports car prize. As Fitch said years later, "We stepped brashly into racing's biggest league and walked off with three prizes on our first try. It was less than we had hoped but more than we deserved."

After the victory, Campbell-Ewald pushed Chevrolet advertising to the redline. Agency writer and racing director Arthur "Barney" Clark prepared an ad for the New York Auto Show program opening just weeks later: "Bring on the hay bales," it cried.

For the July issue of *Road & Track*, he published a stark black-and-white photo of the winning Corvette with its headlights on in the Sebring pits. Walt Hansgen, Fitch's co-driver, was running around the back of the car after a driver change.

"Other people make a luxury car," Clark wrote in a gloves-off slap at Thunderbird, "that has much the same dimensions as this. That's not so tough. And the Europeans make some real rugged competition sports cars—and that's considerably tougher. But nobody but Chevrolet makes a luxury car that's *also* a genuine 100-proof sports car."

In the bleached white sky above the car, this car, the subject of this chapter, Clark created a new legend: "The Real McCoy."

One of the complaints John Fitch and Briggs Cunningham leveled at the car was a lack of fourth gear for high-speed long-distance circuits such as Sebring. This class winner ran a four-speed from ZF.

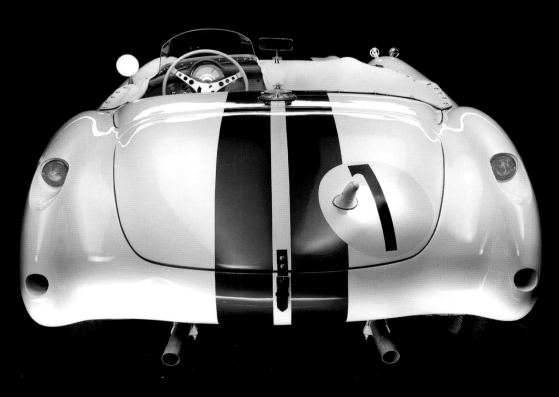

Fitch and co-driver Walt Hansgen finished ninth overall, first in Class B. Sebring race management also awarded Chevrolet the official team prize, and the Corvette team won

1957

XP-64 CORVETTE SUPER SPORT

WHEN RACING TURNED SERIOUS

Zora Arkus-Duntov believed passionately that racing improved the breed. He didn't think necessarily that racing souped-up or modified production cars was as beneficial as others in Chevrolet Division hoped. He admitted years later that "I was not the driving force in the efforts to go racing in the Corvette. I wanted special cars that took the Corvette and went much further." He didn't want a sports car; he wanted a Super Sports car.

On vacation leave in 1954, he had driven a Porsche 550 Spyder in the 24 Hours of Le Mans. He knew intimately how it differed from the company's production 356 and how clearly the racer had evolved from the street car. He competed against Jaguar C-types, racing prototypes derived from the production XK-120s that had inspired the Corvette.

At Sebring in 1956, despite the B-class win that John Fitch and Walt Hansgen accomplished, Duntov and Ed Cole recognized it was not enough. The eight cars that finished ahead of the Corvette were pure-bred racers: Ferraris, Jaguars, an Aston Martin, two Porsche 550s, and a Maserati. Cole had watched the race with design chief Harley Earl and concluded the production Corvette, no matter how well prepared, was no match for specialized single-purpose racers. Perhaps, he wondered, a single-purpose Corvette . . .?

But Cole was no racing director. He was a general manager who worried about starting production of Chevy's new line of trucks and about engineering an all-new 1958 passenger car line. His preoccupation created another opportunity for Earl.

"The original idea was to provoke management," designer Tony Lapine recalled years later. "Harley Earl wanted to provoke management." Earl had done that with a concept vehicle called the Firebird. He felt GM management was ignoring public curiosity about gas turbine power. His staff conceived a delta-wing single-seater and he hinted that Boeing might provide a gas turbine to power it. GM Research Laboratories heard the threat and quickly developed their own turbine for the show car.

"One day we found a dirty white D-type Jaguar waiting for us," Lapine continued. He and Bob Cumberford worked in a well-hidden studio, assigned by Chevrolet studio manager Clare MacKichan, to do odd jobs and new cars. Every studio and room in the building had a name or number. This space, a 20x40-foot windowless chamber, once had been Harley Earl's own work space before he moved into a spacious window-lit office in Styling's administration building. The two designers made a photostat enlargement of a letter "X" and put it on the door.

"Let's use the D-type," Earl told them. "Change the body, drop a Chevy into it. And let's go to Sebring and beat everybody!"

"We had no direction from anybody," Cumberford recalled. "Zora [Duntov] would come in and he and Tony would tell stories." Lapine had raced in Europe, as had Duntov, and Cumberford had designed race cars in California before taking his job at GM. The three men shared a strong interest. So, as Cumberford

__Studio X designers__ Bob Cumberford and Tony Lapine got the assignment to create Chevrolet's sleek sports racer. Harley Earl's goal was to take the car to Le Mans.

An exciting new **EXPERIMENTAL**
Chevrolet Corvette...

Ed Cole approved "production" of one of these in time for a debut at the New York Auto Show in December 1956. He wanted to enter three at Sebring in March, but only this car was complete in time. Jerry Reilly collection

Design and engineering features competed for attention. Designers faired the rearview mirror into the instrument panel, above the simple lever Duntov's engineers installed that adjusted front/rear-brake bias.

put it, "Some tasks, especially racing related, just walked in the door."

Earl had a supporter in this Corvette-Jaguar hybrid with his hand-picked successor Bill Mitchell. They requisitioned an engine from Harry Barr's engineers and word spread quickly. Ed Cole, Barr, Duntov, and Jim Premo, Barr's assistant chief engineer, came for a visit.

"Harley and Bill outlined what they had in mind," Lapine explained. "Cole and Barr just stood there and smiled. Then Zora came over with Jim. We already knew that you couldn't change the body of a D-Jaguar by putting tin snips to structure. It didn't matter that Mister Earl didn't know this. Or that Ed Cole and Harry Barr *did*. Harley accomplished what he set out to do."

Within days, Duntov purchased a Mercedes-Benz 300SL. In Studio X, they removed the body and put the chassis up on steel stands. Then they set a Chevrolet engine, transmission, and differential beside it. Duntov fabricated a tube frame using wooden dowels, duplicating the Mercedes frame around the Chevrolet running gear, short-cutting traditional design, engineering, and development stages.

Duntov knew it was not possible to fit a Corvette engine in the space of the Jaguar engine in the D-type. "You'd have to redo a lot of stuff," Cumberford said, "and Zora didn't want to do that. He wanted his own car. Of course, so did Harley Earl, so the SS came out of that."

Internally the car with its 90-inch wheelbase was known as XP-64, the letters standing for "experimental pursuit," according to Cumberford, an abbreviation Earl adopted from the military during World War II. It represented fighter planes still in development. Cole funded a single car. Duntov, already a master at creative accounting, ordered enough spare pieces to assemble a second car dubbed "the mule." Styling staff skinned the mule in rough fiberglass to evaluate the appearance, wind resistance, and other innovations. The mule's engine developed considerably less horsepower than the aluminum-head 283-cubic-inch V-8 Harry Barr's engineers had fitted with special fuel injection for the actual racer. Earl's sketches, Cumberford's concepts, and Lapine's drawings of the car called for a body of magnesium sheets, while the mule was thick fiberglass. It weighed 150 pounds more, a factor that helped bring out failings in brakes and engine cooling.

GM's Delco-Moraine division was developing disc brakes, but Duntov distrusted anything not yet race proven. So he and his engineering staff developed a kind of anti-lock braking system that used two separate Kelsey-Hayes vacuum servos. He took two pairs of dual-leading shoe center-plane brakes from a 1956 Chrysler and slipped them inside 12-inch-diameter 2.5-inch-wide cast-iron face finned aluminum drums. He mounted them out at the front tires and inboard

Zora Duntov had the luxury of a wind tunnel in late December to test the design for aerodynamic drag and air flow. The results eliminated a hood air intake and guaranteed the shape was as slippery as possible.

If looks could kill, this was a world champion, leaving all other contenders in its wake. Sadly, teething problems in its development, manufacture, and pre-race testing doomed it to early retirement on race day. GM internal politics led to its permanent retirement.

beside the differential at the rear of the car. Pedal pressure modulated the front brakes and he connected the second servo by a pressurized air system to react to the pedal pressure and front brake force, adjusting rear braking to that pressure. He added an inline mercury switch actuated by the car's nose dive during hard braking. Closing the switch shut off the air-pipe, effectively holding the rear brakes at the most recent pressure applied. Without this clever innovation, drivers who increased front brake pressure ensured rear brake lockup, putting directional stability at risk. Duntov's system allowed trail braking later into the turns.

The previous year's 1956 SR models (and two subsequent SR-2 racing cars and one SR-2 styling exercise) retained Chevrolet's solid rear axle suspension. For the SS, Duntov wanted better handling. Engineer Paul Van Valkenburgh explained how Duntov accomplished it: "At the rear . . . things got tricky," he wrote in his book *Chevrolet = Racing . . .?* "A conventional large-diameter de Dion tube connected the rear hubs, bending around behind the Halibrand-derived center-section and inboard brakes. The locating linkage was something new for race cars. It had only four trailing links . . . Oddly enough, all the suspension mount points were rubber-bushed, an unusual practice for any race car."

At the end of 1956, Ed Cole and his racing deputy Walter "Mac" Mackenzie contacted John Fitch again,

asking him to manage the Sebring team for 1957 and co-drive the SS. His work at Sebring the year before, and Dr. Dick Thompson's steady racing with a production convertible through the year, had created a regular production option package of special racing elements, RPO684, which overcame the burdens Fitch encountered a year before. Still, as team manager, Fitch had his work cut out for him. He and Duntov planned for two months of testing. Delays in producing the SS left him three weeks. Duntov's dream was to display one car at the December 1956 New York Auto Show and have three cars racing at Sebring in March. Reality reduced the team to the mule and one finished racer. As Fitch had done in 1956, he tested the mule and applied updates and modifications to the metal-bodied racer. Curious to know how the car compared to the competition, he told writer Mike Knepper in 1989, "I waited for likely prospects [Ferrari, Maserati, Jaguar] on the back straight, and accelerated against them to the end, then followed them through a few of the corners. It was great fun, and very encouraging because the mule compared well with every marque."

Chevrolet had contracted Argentinian grand prix champion Juan Manuel Fangio to drive the car at Sebring. In Friday practice, Fangio and English racer Stirling Moss each drove the fiberglass-bodied mule, Fangio reaching and ultimately qualifying it well up on the grid. But as Harley Earl's stylists put finishing touches on the magnesium-bodied car for its debut at the race, its production ran late enough to pass Fangio's deadline. This released him to join Moss in a Maserati. John Fitch contacted an old friend, Italian grand prix and endurance champion Piero Taruffi in Rome, to fly overnight to join him.

Fangio, Moss, Fitch, and others had driven the mule, and Fitch had hoped to put testing sessions equivalent to two full races under their belts before the main event started. Problems appeared and plagued Duntov and other engineers. When the actual race car reached the track, it was a sprint to overcome its shortcomings.

Balancing the complex braking system proved daunting as it pulled left or right, sometimes locking up a front tire as the system avoided seizing the rears. The higher power of the race motor and the magnesium body's lighter weight required a locking differential to keep the power on the pavement. Coupling this to a de Dion suspension system induced severe axle hop on hard acceleration. Engineers noticed that the cooling radiators barely met their requirements; test drivers complained that the magnesium body trapped the heat of exhaust pipes routed over the two foot wells, roasting the racers and their feet (while the cobbled-together mule, with plenty of holes in its body and seams, was a comfortable racer). Practice sessions presented challenges that required frequent pit stops and furious activities from the engineers. The race introduced all the problems that had not yet appeared.

Race morning, a hot sunny Saturday, March 23, 1957, saw the Corvette SS finished to glorious Motorama show standards. Fitch had done the morning warm-up and came into the pits filled with dread. The braking system that worked well on the mule still was acting up on the racer. Mechanics quickly changed a leaking brake-line fitting. Facing a Le Mans-style run across the track, Fitch rehearsed his jump into the car. He looked up from his efforts and found himself surrounded by photographers and cameramen. Chevrolet's racer was the center of attention. Fitch worried if the blue race car would live up to expectations. As the green flag fell, two production-based Corvettes, the bright red modified SR-2 of Bill Mitchell and the SS, stormed off, encouraging the Chevrolet camp. But soon the sports racing Ferrari

and Maserati entries moved ahead. Fitch started in the SS and pitted on the third lap with a flat-spotted front tire, evidence that the braking system still was troubled. After another six laps, he limped into the pits, a failing condenser cutting out the engine. As he left the pits, a mechanic tossed a few spare parts onto the passenger seat. It was a wise move. On the eleventh lap, the engine died on the circuit. Fitch replaced the ignition coil and solved the problem. The brakes finally became reliable; Fitch had succeeded in bedding them in during the early laps of the race. On lap 21, he pulled in for a scheduled fuel stop and driver change. He warned Taruffi that it felt as if the rear of the car was steering as well as the front. Taruffi accelerated away, beginning the arduous battle to catch up to the leaders. But within two more laps, one of the rear suspension rubber bushings squeezed out of its mount. The rear axle pivoted on every shift and turn, putting the tire in contact with the body and quickly wearing a hole through the thin metal. The SS was so far out of the running that Chevrolet retired it after lap 23. As Fitch described the short race later, "It became more and more doubtful that I would even stay on the road." (The production cars finished twelfth and fifteenth. Mitchell's SR-2 claimed sixteenth. The twelfth-place Dick Thompson/Gaston Andrey car won its class.)

It was a tough day. Before the race, Ed Cole announced that he was considering entering Le Mans, providing two SS cars for Briggs Cunningham's team in June. But Sebring taught everyone that it would take heroic engineering, development, and testing efforts to make the SS competitive on a world stage. The plan stalled, but not only for reasons of logistics and preparation.

Cole was a student of American sensibilities as well as a practitioner of automotive engineering. Organizations like the American Automobile Manufacturers Association (AAMA) and the National Safety Council had found their voices since a horrific race crash in 1955 at Le Mans had killed 80 spectators. They criticized manufacturers promoting car sales through racing, speed, and power boasts. There was perhaps some hypocrisy in the AAMA's concerns; its members included those who raced successfully and those who raced but never won, primarily in NASCAR and other stock car events. On June 7, 1957, the organization spoke:

This board unanimously recommends to the member companies engaged in the manufacture and sale of passenger cars and station wagons that they:

Not participate or engage in any public contest, competitive event, or test of passenger cars involving or suggesting racing or speed, including acceleration tests, or encourage or furnish financial, engineering, manufacturing, advertising, or public relations assistance, or supply 'pace cars' or 'official cars' in connection with any such contest, event, or test, directly or indirectly.

Nor participate or engage in, or encourage or assist employees, dealers, or others to engage in the advertising or publicizing of (a) any race or speed contest, test, or competitive event involving or suggesting speed, whether public or private, involving passengers cars of the results thereof, or (b) the actual or comparative capabilities of passenger cars for speed, or the specific engine size, torque, horsepower, or ability to accelerate or perform in any context that suggests speed.

Among all these words, the key was "recommends" in the first paragraph quoted here. The AAMA and its members had done this to stave off interest in auto safety that was emerging in Congress. Legislation forced on them was something none of them desired. The announcement had no legal standing; it was not a mandate. But who among the manufacturers wanted to be seen as flaunting safety? They all had agreed, and they all immediately moved their racing operations from the front of the building to somewhere near the back door.

Underneath its paper-thin magnesium skin, the SS was a hastily copied blend of the Mercedes-Benz 300SL and Jaguar D-type chassis design. The body was another blend, of function and beauty.

The 24 Hours of Le Mans took place 15 days after the AAMA recommendation. When the checkered flag fell in France on June 23, five Jaguar D-types and a Ferrari prototype took the first six places. No Corvettes were there. Little had happened to the mule and the pale blue magnesium-bodied SS since Sebring, but in late June they were cleaned up and moved into storage.

In late 1958, design director Bill Mitchell pulled the mule from storage. He had purchased it from Cole for $1. He set up another small studio and asked Larry Shinoda to design a new body for it so he could race it. Shinoda adapted concepts that fellow designers Chuck Pohlmann, Peter Brock, and others had developed for a future production Corvette. Mitchell, an avid deep sea fisherman, dubbed his new racer the Sting Ray.

The blue Corvette SS race car remained in storage until 1967, when it joined the permanent collection at the Indianapolis Motor Speedway Hall of Fame Museum. It is regularly on display there.

1959

CHEVROLET EXPERIMENTAL RESEARCH VEHICLE I

4

REDEFINING THE EXPERIMENT

There were many perspectives on the 1957 SS after its run at Sebring. Accountants felt the money had been squandered. Management sensed the failure of the sleek blue car had hurt Chevrolet's image. Public relations ignored the SS and boasted Chevrolet had won a second time at Sebring (in its class). But Duntov and a number of other engineers saw it as a success: They had learned what would work and what would not.

One question that arose with the magnesium-bodied SS was how to deal with the unexpectedly brutal cockpit heat. Through 1957, 1958, and into early 1959, Duntov wrestled with the problem. What about putting the engine behind the driver?

The AAMA recommendation to stop racing became the public face of U.S. automakers through 1957 and 1958. If private teams chose to compete with their cars, of course there was little GM, Ford, or Chrysler could do about that. However, by 1959, corporate fears had relaxed and the chilled atmosphere had begun to thaw.

For the 1959 calendar year, Chevrolet introduced the Corvair, a rear-engined economy car. Chevrolet had plans to elevate its performance, handling, and image into something far sportier. It would never compete with the Corvette because product planners meant it always to have four seats. But it offered possibilities for the engineers.

Maurice Olley had retired and Robert Schilling replaced him as head of General Motors Research & Development. Schilling imported Duntov for chassis

and handling and another engineer, Frank Winchell, for powertrain and transmissions in January 1959. Winchell had overseen development of the Corvair transaxle and Schilling put both men to work on a proposed project called the "Q" car. This was to be a passenger automobile with a front engine, a rear-mounted transmission (or trans-axle), and an independent suspension. While Duntov was assigned to Schilling and R&D, his heart still pulsed with Corvette motivation. He quickly envisioned a rear- or mid-engined Corvette that would use Winchell's transaxle.

He visited Bill Mitchell, a performance addict who started his design staff creating hundreds of concept sketches followed by several full-size clay models of the "Q" Corvette. Budget considerations killed Chevrolet's "Q" sedan and this took down the funding (and justification) for any application as small as the Corvette production run. (Pontiac's compact Tempest, introduced in 1961, made use of "Q"-car development work with a front engine and rear transaxle, earning it *Motor Trend* magazine's "Car of the Year" award.)

Duntov, with an obsession that was his hallmark personality trait, was undeterred. Working in R&D simply gave him the venue to further his mid-engine ideas. As Paul Van Valkenburgh recalled in his book *Chevrolet = Racing . . .?* "The best rationalization [Duntov] could come up with was a research vehicle for testing tires, independent rear suspensions, and vehicle dynamics in general."

The car started life with an aluminum-block 283 V-8 that developed 353 horsepower. By 1964, engineers had replaced it with this 377-cubic-inch aluminum V-8 with Hilborn fuel injection at 500-plus horsepower.

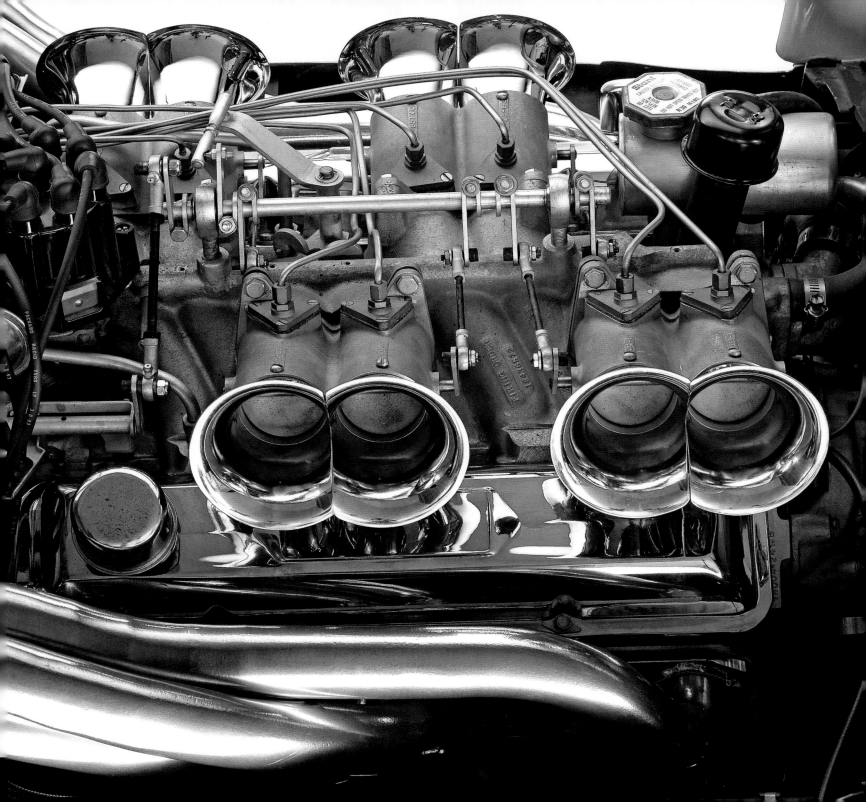

It's clear GM took pride in Zora Duntov and his experiments. The long view makes it clear GM simply didn't know what to do with what he created. Conflicts between a corporate policy discouraging racing and many of its divisions secretly supporting it must have given corporate officers ulcers. Jerry Reilly collection

For several years, CERV 1 did serve as a tire test mule in the race to bring wider tires to production street vehicles. Tires that Firestone and Goodyear introduced in 1968 resulted from extraordinary cornering and traction forces the CERV provided.

Even after assembling the blue racer SS and the fiberglass mule, engineering had enough spare parts on hand to develop an all-new car. Duntov and his senior engineers Harold Krieger and Walt Zetye mated an engine and four-speed transmission directly to the differential. Believing that racing was less of a career-ending pursuit than it had been two years earlier, the three men designed the car to meet Indianapolis 500 regulations. They conceived a mid-engine single-seater on a 96-inch wheelbase. They established front and rear tire track—and the car's maximum body width—at 56 inches. Overall length stretched to just 172 inches.

As a tire and suspension test vehicle, Duntov gave some thought to running the car at Pikes Peak, a concept that provoked some on his development team to nickname the car "the hillclimber." Stylist Larry Shinoda and designer Tony Lapine devised the minimalist lines for the efficient bodywork that encased the tube frame and accompanying mechanicals.

Duntov carried over the SS front suspension, including the variable-rate coil springs. Coming off the transaxle, he used the half-shafts as upper links in a multi-link fully independent rear configuration. This took the "Q" concept a step further. In its iteration after this, it appeared on production Corvettes beginning in 1963.

The engine was even more intriguing. Engineers working for Harry Barr and Jim Premo had experimented with all-aluminum engines. They cast a series of new 283-cubic-inch V-8 cylinder blocks from a high silicon-content alloy that did not need cylinder bore liners. Aluminum heads topped the engine and engineers produced aluminum water pump housings, flywheels, clutch pressure plates, and starter motor bodies. According to Karl Ludvigsen in *Corvette: America's Star Spangled Sports Car*, this block weighed 90 pounds less than the comparable 283 cast-iron version. With a Rochester fuel injection intake system in place, the engine developed 353 horsepower. It made for a very potent automobile at 1,450-pounds.

Design and development continued on the CERV (Chevrolet Experimental Research Vehicle) through early 1960 although Duntov stepped away regularly to work on one or another project in R&D and to collaborate with Briggs Cunningham on his effort to campaign three production Corvettes at Le Mans for the June 24-hour race. So it was not until early September 1960 that Duntov got "the hillclimber" to the hill.

Winter came early that year and it was snowing on Pikes Peak above 10,000 feet. Because racers

Duntov's interest in mid- and rear-engine placement came from two sources. He was curious about how the change in balance would affect or improve handling, and he wanted to relocate the intense source of heat from in front of the driver.

were unable to run to the 14,000 foot summit, they only could time segments and compare those to what observers recalled of other racers and their performances. Memories were fuzzy. Duntov had offered the car to Firestone, which enthusiastically planned tire development runs in the car. But that interest evaporated when the series of elapsed times through various segments appeared slow.

Back in Michigan where he could match real data, Duntov learned that "the time was really splendid," he told Karl Ludvigsen, "and on every stretch I was knocking off time from the record." Prior to leaving Detroit, they had leased Continental Divide Raceway in Colorado for the Firestone tests. After the Pikes Peak runs but before understanding their accomplishment, they went ahead with the tire tests in order to recoup some value from the trip. Engineers wisely had brought along Halibrand wheels in a dozen sizes.

"Firestone worked with Zora [Duntov] on the tires," Ludvigsen wrote, summarizing the trip. The tire maker's first problem was trying to get suitable tires on the rear that could handle the car's acceleration and handling potential. "CERV I became an important experimental tool for both Firestone and Goodyear in the development of the modern wider tire" (which first appeared in 1968).

The car's public debut came a few weeks later at Riverside International Raceway in early November on the weekend of the U.S. Grand Prix. Stirling Moss and Dan Gurney put in laps, topping out at 170 miles per hour on Riverside's long back straight. They each lapped the 3.3-mile circuit at a pace just nine seconds off the lap record that Moss had set in a Lotus during practice.

For Duntov, 170 wasn't fast enough. Earlier in the year, NASCAR founder Bill France had pledged $10,000 to reward the first 180-mile-per-hour lap of his 2.5-mile banked track. Duntov knew the car needed more horsepower for the higher speed. In Detroit, working through 1962 and into 1963, engineers mounted and tested a GMC 4-53 supercharger

Duntov and senior engineers *Walt Zetye and Harold Krieger created a vehicle they claimed was for testing tires and independent suspensions. The fact that its dimensions, including its 96-inch wheelbase, met Indianapolis 500 regulations was not a coincidence.*

and then Thompson-Ramo-Woodridge turbochargers. While the blower developed 420 horsepower, the twin turbos boosted output to 500.

Engineers worked with Lapine and Shinoda to create a new nose. This one replaced the side intakes at the front suspension with long fairings leading back to the front suspension pieces. Engine developers replaced the 283 with a new 377-cubic-inch block. They mounted Hilborn fuel injection on a cross-ram manifold. On a cold morning in March 1964, Duntov fired up the new engine and headed out onto the 4.5-mile five-lane banked circular track at GM's proving ground in Milford, Michigan. When he completed the run,

his sleek, simple unique CERV I—the subject of this chapter—had lapped the circle at an average speed of 206 miles per hour.

The car led a much more sedate life until 1972, when Chevrolet donated the car to the Briggs Cunningham Museum in Costa Mesa, California. When Cunningham closed his museum in 1987, Florida collector Miles Collier acquired the entire collection. He sold CERV I to collectors Steve Hendrickson of Minnesota and K. D. James of Houston. Some years later, Mike Yager, founder of Mid America Motorworks, acquired the car for his collection. It is on display at his MY Garage Museum at his corporate headquarters in Effingham, Illinois.

On a cold morning in March 1964, Zora Duntov climbed into this cockpit at GM's proving ground at Milford, Michigan. He fired up the V-8 and headed out on the banked circular track, lapping 206 miles per hour by the time he was finished.

Larry Shinoda and Tony Lapine designed the minimalist lines and shapes. The efficient bodywork encased a tube frame and front and rear louvers extracted radiator and engine heat.

1960

CUNNINGHAM No. 3

TAKING ON THE REST OF THE WORLD

French racing enthusiasts loved Briggs Cunningham. So did *L'Automobile Club de l'Ouest* (ACO), France's Automobile Club of the West, which organized and ran the 24-hour race at Le Mans. For several years, beginning in 1950 with his Cadillac "Sedan de Ville" coupe and his wondrous "Cadillac Spyder" nicknamed "le Monstre," Cunningham had raced interesting and sometimes entertaining automobiles there. The Cadillacs and then his Cunningham C2R, C4R, and C5R models were the first American-manufactured racers to appear since a Duesenberg had run in 1935. In 1953, and again in 1954, Cunningham roadsters finished third overall.

Ed Cole and Zora Duntov loved Cunningham as well. As a private entrant, he could take Corvettes into competition, something no GM employees could do because of the AAMA recommendation against racing.

Chevrolet had disappointed the French race management in 1957. Cole, Duntov, and John Fitch had entered three Corvettes to the June race. The AAMA's edict, which GM's chairman Harlow "Red" Curtice hurriedly signed, cancelled that commitment. The ACO was alert to public concerns and criticisms of too much power, too-large engines, and too-high speeds. In response, the organization limited engine displacement on prototypes and Grand Touring (GT) cars to three liters (183 cubic inches) for the 1958 and 1959 events. They increased the limit to five liters (305 cubic inches) for 1960, but only for GT cars. Briggs Cunningham

inquired about entering and organizers hurried an application to him, inviting him to bring as many as four cars.

Cunningham shipped three Corvettes fitted with Chevy's 283-cubic-inch V-8 (plus a prototype Jaguar) to Long Island, New York, to shops run by Alfred Momo. Duntov showed up to direct, assist, and make recommendations, accompanied by Frank Burrell, a Cadillac engineer who coincidentally had vacationed at Le Mans during the race weekend in June 1950. Momo's staff bolted hardtop roofs onto the Corvettes, removed the chrome trim and the grille inserts, and mounted large gas tanks with refueling notches in the rear window. Powerful driving and fog lamps, color-keyed headlight covers to help lap-time keepers differentiate between cars, and an understated white-with-blue-stripes paint scheme finished off the cars' appearance. Under the hood, Duntov wanted to use new aluminum cylinder heads from Chevrolet Engineering's R&D labs to the 4.6-liter engines. But Momo did not trust them and Cunningham honored his manager's decision to simply enlarge valves and improve intake and exhaust flow. Duntov had devised a system that used an electric pump to surge cooling oil through its own radiator, and these went on the cars.

Momo's work slimmed the cars down to 2,980 pounds while a fourth Corvette entry from Lucky Casner's Camoradi team tipped the scales at 2,830 pounds. The late Bob Grossman recalled Cunningham's

Chevrolet had entered three Corvette SS models in the 1957 Le Mans race but had to withdraw following the AAMA recommendation. Cunningham took three well-modified production cars and got John Fitch and Bob Grossman to drive this one.

preparation in an interview in Albert Bochroch's classic book on the French race, *Americans at LeMans.*

"Cunningham really knew how to organize a team," Grossman told Bochroch. "A couple of months before Le Mans, Briggs rented Bridgehampton [circuit on eastern Long Island], and we took the cars up there and ran them hard. We practiced and practiced and the wheels kept breaking. Finally Briggs [Cunningham] had to get a bunch of special wheels." Duntov's much-favored Halibrand knock-off wheels returned to Corvette racers.

Le Mans organizers typically staged a practice session on the course in mid-April. The circuit raced along public roads regularly travelled by cars, buses, tractors, and trucks in normal times and this was the one opportunity for teams and drivers to test new vehicles. Cunningham and Momo were uncertain of the quality of gas they would get at the track and so they made a strategic decision. According to Jesse Alexander's account in the October 1960 issue of *Sports Cars Illustrated*, Cunningham let his drivers "deliberately blow an engine in practice to see just what liberties they could take on the gas available. The result," Alexander wrote, "was that the cars were reliable enough but were not really sufficiently fast to be impressive for their engine size."

Size proved to be both a benefit and a drawback. The race started at 4 p.m. on Saturday, June 25, with a typical field of 55 cars. A few minutes before 6 p.m., a hard rain covered the course. Arriving in a squall, the downpour flooded parts of the track, forcing several cars off course. Alexander's race report continued:

"The Cunningham/Kimberley car [No. 1] went out early when Kimberley got into a sudden spot of rain and was just a bit too fast. The car swapped ends before he could do a thing and was smashed up considerably, even starting a fire in the engine room." The car rolled over and Bill Kimberley scrambled out before the fire erupted.

Rain continued through the night but the two other team cars persevered. As John Fitch recalled in a recent interview, he and co-driver Bob Grossman (in car No. 3), and No. 2 car driven by Dick Thompson and Fred Windridge, kept a steady pace. The Corvettes held traction as the heavy cars and their narrow tires sluiced through the rain-soaked track. The four drivers took turns holding off challengers and they

improved their positions through the night. Despite the downpour, 30 entrants still were running at 10 a.m. the next morning.

The rain and lower temperatures gave the Corvettes another break. Slower paces through the night kept the engines cooler. This advantage evaporated once the weather passed and the pace resumed. Duntov's pressurized oil-cooling concept was not enough to keep the cars from overheating.

"[The] saddest Corvette mishap of all affected the Windridge/Thompson car," Jesse Alexander wrote. "After a crash slashed away many square feet of its bodywork and left the car in the sand early in the race Saturday afternoon, Thompson lost more than an hour digging the car out. "It ran beautifully," Alexander continued, "till noon on Sunday when suddenly—as Windridge passed the pits—a huge cloud of smoke poured out of the exhaust as the engine blew. Shortage of oil was the basic reason." Le Mans rules that year allowed fuel stops anytime a driver or team wanted. But crew members could add oil and water only after 25 laps—about 215 miles—has passed since the previous replenishment.

Bernard Cahier, writing in the October 1960 issue of *Road & Track*, put the race in context: "Le Mans without last minute drama wouldn't be Le Mans and, as the last two hours began ticking away, things began to happen." Around 2:30 p.m. Sunday, 90 minutes before the checkered flag, John Fitch babied Corvette No. 3 into the pits badly overheating.

"There was . . . plenty of 'cooling-off' excitement in the Cunningham pits, where Fitch's Corvette came in boiling time after time," Cahier wrote. "The car was so hot that it was refusing to start, so, to cool the engine more quickly, someone had the bright idea of bringing buckets of ice cubes. These were scattered all over the engine under the critical and disgusted eyes of Zora Duntov, the well-known chief engineer of Chevrolet Corvette."

Duntov was not yet chief engineer, but he may have indeed been critical and disgusted. Or perhaps he was just frustrated and disappointed. The quick-thinking "someone" with the bright idea was one of Cunningham's team mechanics, Willy Frick, who raided Cunningham's luxurious and well-stocked camper parked behind his pits. Before the engine temperature soared, Fitch and Grossman had climbed

This car's brilliant amber fog lamps illuminated the pillars inside one of the buildings at Carlisle Show Grounds in Pennsylvania. Ahead, the cool blue light of day awaited outside the large door.

to fourth place overall, holding back six or seven Ferrari Berlinettas challenging their car for the finish. The coolant refill rule was tough, but another regulation drastically revised the strategy that Cunningham and Momo had created for the weekend: To be classified at the end of the race as a "finisher," the car had to complete four laps in the final hour. Through the wet night, Fitch and Grossman had circulated the course in 5 minutes 15 seconds and they had qualified the car in 4 minutes 28.3 seconds. As Bochroch reported, "Every lap, No. 3 would ease in, get iced up and gingerly crawl away, taking about 15 minutes to complete the lap and ice up again."

Around the track a crowd estimated at 250,000 learned of the plight of No. 3 from the public address system and they yelled encouragement as the car negotiated the circuit at a sedate pace. Across from Cunningham's pits, spectators cheered the ice packing effort. Every 15 minutes the white-and-blue car steamed into the pits to the huge roar of the fans. Moments later it moved steadily back out on course to the sound of even louder support.

Mercifully the anxiety ended at 4 p.m. A 3-liter Ferrari Testa Rosa prototype had won the race. Another Testa Rosa came in second, followed by an Aston Martin sports racer and then four of the Ferrari

Alfred Momo's efforts reduced little weight from production cars to this racer. The large fuel tank and center-mounted large filler plus the roll bar and driving lights slimmed the Le Mans entries to 2,980 pounds from 2,985 pounds for street cars.

Cunningham's team manager, Alfred Momo, *enlarged intake and exhaust valves on the 283-cubic-inch V-8, improving intake and exhaust flow. Duntov developed 315-horsepower cast-aluminum cylinder heads, but Momo chose to not risk unproven parts on a long race.*

Berlinetta 3-liter GT cars that ultimately roared past Fitch. Ferrari had dominated the event, claiming six of the seven top places. Corvette No. 3 steamed across the finish in eighth place overall. It took first in the Grand Touring under 5,000cc class.

Following the race in France, Cunningham brought No. 3 and his other two entries back to the United States. He sold all three cars. Number 3 disappeared into club racing and, after a season or two, its owner converted the car to street use. It changed hands several times and fell off most people's radar. Corvette restorer and racing historian Kevin Mackay in New York and Carlisle Events

founder (the late) Chip Miller in Pennsylvania spent a couple of years searching for the car, which Miller finally acquired in 2000. Then Mackay commenced a long careful research and restoration process at his Corvette Repair Inc. on Long Island. It was Miller's goal to reunite the car and Fitch at Le Mans in June 2010 for the fiftieth anniversary of its class win there.

In the meanwhile, Cunningham No. 3, the subject of this chapter, resides in the Miller family collection, where it remains the big winner in the hearts and souls of French and American racing enthusiasts for nearly half a century.

Deep upholstered bucket seats held John Fitch or Bob Grossman into place behind the wheel. A large tachometer replaced the stock semicircular speedometer on the instrument panel.

6

1960
TASCO TURQUOISE CONVERTIBLE

SEARCHERS GONE TO LOOK FOR AMERICA

Actor Martin Milner was one of those celebrities at whom Chevrolet aimed the 1953 Corvette. Herbert B. "Bert" Leonard was an even bigger target. Leonard had risen through television's ranks to become an executive producer, the man who developed and ran successful and popular series shows. In late 1953 he introduced a drama starring a German shepherd and a young boy, called *The Adventures of Rin Tin Tin*. Milner had appeared in television's *Dragnet*, and other series and films through the early and mid-1950s. Neither of them, however, was impressed enough to pay much attention to the car until they had to.

In writing schools, instructors teach young talents to "write what you know." A slice of Leonard's life, of what he knew from his youth, grew into a very popular series. In a 1982 interview in *Emmy* magazine with film writer Richard Maynard, Bert recalled a lunch with his friend, *Naked City* writer Stirling Silliphant in 1959 while that show was in production. As a child in New York, Leonard had a much wealthier friend who was a prep school student. Over lunch he and Silliphant imagined what it might have been like to hit the roads in his friend's sports car. An idea gelled immediately and by the time lunch was over, they had their show name, *The Searchers*, and a pilot story roughed out. Leonard and Silliphant had created an idea that took another popular TV series of the mid-1950s *Wagon Train* into the next decade. In their proposal, they wrote:

The theme – search, unrest, uncertainty, seeking answers, looking for a way of life.

The people – are young enough to appeal to the youthful audience, old enough to be involved in adult situations.

The stories – will be about something, [Italics were Silliphant's] will be honest, and will face up to life, look for and suggest meanings, things people can identify with, and yet there will be the romance and escape of young people with wanderlust.

The locales – the whole width and breadth of the U.S., with stories shot in the actual locations, a la Naked City. *What we did for one city, we now propose to do for a country and for many of its industries and businesses.*

In late 1959, Leonard and Silliphant pitched this idea to Columbia-Screen Gems. They were an acknowledged success; *Naked City* had established new standards for storytelling and cinematography in television. This idea, however, was different. As Screen Gems executives explained when they rejected the series initially, this was "about two bums on the road."

The Searchers verged on late 1950s European Existentialism, a philosophy that questioned why humans exist. Because he suspected this was a bit too deep for television executives at the time, Silliphant brought it back to more comfortable territory. He

For the first season of the show, *Chevrolet provided producer Herbert B. Leonard two Tasco Turquoise convertibles. This excellent-condition survivor is an unrestored original, though not from the series. No records exist of the whereabouts of the show cars.*

concluded their pitch by promising that each episode would be "packed with at least two or three top-staged brawls (built into the character of Buz)." To demonstrate his faith in the idea, Leonard funded the pilot himself. In exchange, if Columbia bought the show, he would own 80 percent of the series.

Screen Gems execs reminded Leonard and Silliphant that New York's Broadway had recently staged a play titled *The Searchers,* so the pair adopted the name of America's emotionally-laden "mother road," *Route 66.*

Regular viewers know that the 115 episodes over four years rarely found stories along U.S. Highway 66. That mattered only to those obsessed with detail. Leonard's crew shot the pilot, called "The Wolf Tree," in Concord, Kentucky, calling it the fictional Garth, Alabama, in February 1960. The show debuted on a Friday night, October 7, 1960, with the episode renamed "Black November." By then the production crew was leapfrogging across the country. Leonard, Silliphant, and a production assistant scouted areas that gave them several nearby towns around which to craft two

or three episodes. Four weeks later, the production caravan arrived and began filming. Silliphant sometimes wrote from hotel rooms near the locations, delivering script pages that day to the waiting cast, each story faithfully adhering to his promise to show America, its industries and its businesses, and a fist fight or two thrown in for good measure.

The premise of the show was that Tod Stiles, played by Martin Milner, had just lost his father, a New York City shipping company owner. Stiles, a junior at Yale, educated and thoughtful, well-bred and polite, came home for the funeral to discover a bankrupt business and a legacy that included nothing more than a new 1960 Corvette convertible.

"I've been seriously wrong about a lot of things in my life," Milner admitted in an interview in 1998. "And I said to Bert Leonard, 'A Corvette isn't that exciting a car. Why don't we do this in a Ferrari?'" Milner laughed.

"'Well,' Bert said to me, 'we've got a pretty good chance of getting sponsorship from Chevrolet. And there's a pretty good chance of not getting anything from Ferrari.'"

In an interview in 1963, writer Silliphant told the interviewer that Route 66 was "a search for identity in contemporary America." If any two people had to go off to find themselves in America, there was no better tool, then or now.

Milner related this story to documentary producer John Paget while they were completing a retrospective two-hour show tracing the actual route of Route 66. For that production Milner drove a 1960 Roman Red convertible (with white coves), which gave rise to yet another of the countless myths about the television series.

An actor Leonard had used and liked on *Naked City*, George Maharis, was hired even before Milner to play a dockside employee named Buz Murdoch. Maharis' character Buz was a native of New York City's Hell's Kitchen, streetwise and cynical, equally quick to react or to joke. Now Buz was jobless. Suddenly uprooted in every sense, the two clean-cut handsome young men, friends from summers working on Stiles' docks, took off to find themselves.

"Tod says," Maharis announced in that first episode, written by Silliphant, "if we keep moving we'll find a place to plant roots . . .. But with me, it's fine just moving."

Screen Gems and CBS picked up the series, and listings in publications such as *TV Guide* identified Milner and Maharis as the principal players. But

there were four stars apparent to those who watched the show carefully: Maharis, Milner, the Corvette (often written in to Silliphant's scripts as a character itself), and The Road Across America. As television historian Mark Alvey wrote in *The Road Movie Book*, "*Route 66* is a tale both of search and flight, and as a serial narrative characteristic of American commercial television, its central meaning lies not in some finite goal at the end of the road, but in the discoveries made along the way."

The show's travels rooted much of America to their television sets every Friday for four seasons. The audience's vicarious restlessness brought Chevrolet back year after year as principal sponsor. "See the U.S.A. in your Chevrolet," was more than an advertising jingle for this show—it was close as existentialism was to being the show's philosophical foundation.

Chevrolet's advertising agency's Los Angeles office provided Leonard a pair of Tasco Turquoise blue convertibles. As Leonard and Silliphant had promised, the show hit the road and travelled . . . and travelled. Maharis recalled recently that they covered 40,000

Chevrolet assembled 635 convertibles in Tasco Turquoise, three pairs of which saw film duty on the show. Originally titled The Searchers, producer Leonard promised stories that would be "honest." But to sell it to CBS, writer Stirling Silliphant had to promise at least one good fist fight in every episode.

Chevrolet introduced the quad headlights in the 1958 models, and many design features remained unchanged through the 1962 cars. The TV show's director of photography Jack Marta complained about the challenge of lighting the actors' faces against a sky-blue car. So for subsequent seasons, Chevrolet provided Corvettes in Fawn Beige.

miles each year. Production manager Sam Manners ran a road train, as he explained to show historian James Rosin. A transporter carried the two Corvettes as well as a Chapman Crane, a truck with an arm capable of lifting the camera nearly 50 feet in the air. A station wagon supported the camera for moving front shots; a Corvair missing its front trunk lid served as camera car for rear views. Another dozen vehicles made up the convoy with portable dressing rooms, costumes, and the camera equipment, lenses, lighting gear, and generators cinematographer Jack Marta needed to get each episode on film.

For Chevrolet, it was the natural "vehicle" to promote their sports car. Similar motives attracted GM executives and viewers: There was no need to wait for a vacation to see the country in the family station wagon—hopefully a Chevy. Every week millions of individuals went on an adventure, imagining themselves as the third (or fourth or fifth) rider stuffed into the Corvette between Buz and Tod.

The show provided adventure, with Tod, Buz, and the Corvette as tour guides. Events, tumultuous and timely, befell the two young men just as they arrived in one locale or another. Silliphant, a writer profoundly in sync with America's psyche, steered them to women's rights, racial inequality, corporate malfeasance, land and water rights, international espionage, murder, theft, assault, marital and familial discord, war crimes, revolutionary terrorists, drug addiction and abuse, the role of the government in an individual's rights, and the responsibilities of an individual to a town or nation. The episodes were self-contained, an anthology type of storytelling that introduced conflicts involving guest stars outside the Corvette. By the time the sleek luggage-encumbered convertible left town, all was right with the world and it was time to move on.

In an interview in *Time* magazine in August 1963, Silliphant said, "The meaning of Route 66 has to do with 'a search for identity in contemporary America. It is a show about a statement of existence. If anything,

It's easy to imagine getting your kicks on Route 66 in a car like this. While bandleader Bobby Troupe wrote the famous song, producer Leonard called on film-score writer Nelson Riddle for the music for the series.

it is closer to Sartre and Kafka than to anything else. We are terribly serious, and we feel that life contains a certain amount of pain.'"

The show caused some pain for cinematographer Marta, who worked hard to illuminate actors' faces in bright sunlight against a pale blue car that reflected so much light. For the 1961–1962 season, the Campbell-Ewald agency provided the show with Fawn Beige convertibles. That darker color choice remained through 1964, when the series ended.

Some viewers picked up the difference between the tones of the cars, even filmed in black-and-white. They noticed that each year the seemingly penniless Stiles and Murdock (who often said they took jobs just for gas money) travelled in a current model Corvette. That question fit right in with, "How can they be in Maine if the show is called *Route 66*?"

As a title, *The Searchers* was not "catchy," just as a Ferrari convertible would have been unbelievable—why wouldn't Tod sell a car like that and go back to Yale?

The simple facts: 283 cubic inches, 290 horsepower, 2,985 pounds. Corvette had introduced the Rochester fuel injection in 1957; it was a $484.20 option by 1960.

But Dad's two-seat American-made Corvette enticed the two young men onto the road, letting Stiles search for roots and Murdock keep moving without taking much baggage or other passengers.

Chevrolet's design studio began planning updates to the Corvette's first-generation body even before introduction in 1953. Poor sales slipped the redesign back from the 1956 to 1958, when quad headlights appeared. Stylists Peter Brock, Chuck Pohlman, and others slaved away on the "next" Corvette, first called the "Q" and then nicknamed just "the next one." In 1961 the car received a new rear end that hinted at The Next One. Quad headlights stayed through 1962 season and subsequent generations. The Sting Ray showed up for the 1962–1963 season and a new one carried on for the 1963–1964 programs.

About every 3,000 miles, Campbell-Ewald replaced the show's cars, reconditioning them and sending them off to friendly dealers to sell as "executive" vehicles. Sam Manners remembered running though three or four cars per season. With each season's renewal, new models arrived in time for the caravan to leave L.A. By 1963, that road show had grown to fifty vehicles on the road covering 40,000 miles each year. By then Chevrolet provided Corvettes to Milner and Maharis, Manners, and others for personal use as well.

The car shown here is not a vehicle from the show. Its white coves betray it, as does its unrestored survivor status. Pennsylvania owner Mike Nardo and his father know the history of the car and it did not include television stardom. But Nardo's car is a survivor with 37,000 miles, a four-speed transmission, and the same factory steel wheels and wheel covers that Tod ended up with after Episode 22. In that show, "Eleven, The Hard Way," the two men helped a small town confront the risks of gambling in order to save itself. To stake a loan to the town's auditor in a make-or-break game of dice, Tod sold the wire wheels that drove the car through two-thirds of the premiere season.

The show itself was a gamble. There are reports that CBS didn't care for it. Network president Jim Aubrey complained to Leonard that the show was "too downbeat," and that he wanted more "broads, bosoms, and fun." But, as Leonard told Mark Alvey, Chevrolet "liked the hard hitting show they bought . . . They

wanted the reality, the drama, and the movement; not the sexy women and cliché characters." GM's marketing studies revealed that the show attracted huge audiences of young people between the age of 10 and 14, a prime target then and now. The show ran for four seasons, surviving the disappearance of co-star Maharis who was suffering with hepatitis brought on by the exhausting pace of travel and six-day shooting weeks. Milner drove on, searching for roots and meaning. The show finally slowed to a halt months after Glenn Corbett, playing Lincoln Case, replaced a still-ailing Maharis. "Linc" was more like Tod than Buz and the interplay and counterpoint that worked so well with Maharis and Milner never reappeared.

Critics have analyzed the show's writing, its acting, and its stories. Some have compared it to beatnik author Jack Kerouac's seminal travel story *On the Road*. Kerouac sued Silliphant and Leonard, accusing them of plagiarism. But as Paul Goodman explained in his book *Growing up Absurd*, "The entire action of *On the Road* is the avoidance of interpersonal conflict." *Route 66* was precisely the opposite, and viewer surveys commissioned in 1961 by Chevrolet and other sponsors learned that the audience understood the role of the stars as knights in shining armor, riding in week after week to save damsels—or entire towns—in distress. It is their co-star in this noble pursuit, their trusty steed, their white charger—well, first blue and then beige—that is the subject of this chapter.

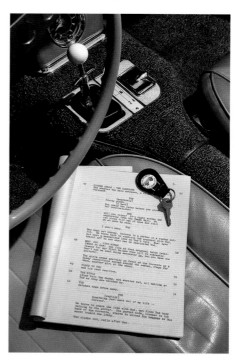

Stirling Silliphant's scripts treated the Corvette as a third character. The car was a fully-involved partner in getting the two lead characters into new towns right when something was about to happen.

Headed for action, *George Maharis and Martin Milner leapt from their Tasco Turquoise convertible. For the first season, Chevrolet provided cars in this color, which challenged the cinematographer.* The Everett Collection, Inc.

For four television seasons, *George Maharis (in foreground) as Buz Murdock, and Martin Milner, playing Tod Stiles, traveled all over America in search of a place to call home. Chevrolet, sponsors of the series* Route 66, *exchanged models annually and replaced "picture cars" every 3,000 miles or so.* The Everett Collection, Inc.

1961
BM/SP

ADVANCING THE LEGEND A QUARTER-MILE AT A TIME

Before he even could drive, John Mazmanian owned a car. He'd spent $25 and bought a 1930 Model A coupe in 1940 when he was 14 and in junior high school. For the next several months, he went completely through the car with the school's auto shop instructor. By the time he got to Garfield High School in East Los Angeles, the A was gone, replaced by a 1939 Mercury with a chopped top. Before going to college for mechanical engineering, he had a 1932 Ford highboy roadster that he'd raced on L.A.'s east side as a member of the Gophers Car Club and had taken out to El Mirage Dry Lake north of Los Angeles. The car hit 118 miles per hour on the sand, a run duly recorded by the Southern California Timing Association (SCTA). Right after the attack on Pearl Harbor, John enlisted in the U.S. Navy and served in the Pacific.

Home from the war, John married and stepped into his family's waste disposal business. But even with a growing family and business responsibilities, John, who stood 6 feet 5 inches tall and had long ago earned the nickname Big John, couldn't let go of his interest in performance cars. Looking for a family sedan in 1957, he found a Ford Fairlane with a factory supercharged 312 V-8. It chauffeured the family on weekdays but on weekends, Big John worked on the car and hit the streets.

His hobby grew and he added other cars, working on them nights and weekends, and painting them Candy Apple Red, a favorite color and one that became as much a logo as his stature. His grandson Nick said

recently that Big John "resembled John Wayne in my mind because 'The Duke' always walked to the beat of his own drum and my grandfather did the same." Success followed John on the streets and the new drag strips opening up all over southern California. Other parts of the United States had racing, but the L.A. area, with its year-round racing season, became home to specialty shops and new organizations hoping to improve the quality of racing for participants and spectators. The network of fast racers and those who could help them spread rapidly.

In those days, C.S. Mead Chevrolet was the working home for a couple of serious racing enthusiasts. Service manager Bill Thomas owned and campaigned one of the first 1957 Corvette racers to reach the West Coast and one of his service technicians, Don Nicholson, ran the dynamometer for the dealership. Big John stopped in one day in the fall of 1960 and learned from "Dyno Don" that one of the fuel-injected Corvettes on the lot had tested considerably better that the other cars they had. John bought the car that day.

"Knowing my grandfather," Nick Mazmanian recalled, "the car had every option available . . . if it wasn't high-end, it wasn't worth squat."

When John wasn't working on the family business, he was working on his cars. The Corvette saw a few races and John learned how strong it was. Still, there were other cars in the garage and other ideas in his

By the time "Big John" Mazmanian retired this drag racer, he'd seen it reach 130 miles per hour in the quarter-mile, in an elapsed time of 10.9 seconds. A GMC 6-71 supercharger tops the engine.

An opportunity to race with Dragmaster *10.00x16 slicks at San Gabriel Dragstrip set the crew to work with a hacksaw to open up the rear wheel wells. At that point, Big John removed the grille and installed a small Moon fuel tank up front and redesigned the hood cut out again.*

mind, so he never removed its radio or its heater. "It wasn't until he found out his nineteen-year-old nephew, Rich [Siroonian] was taking the car out and racing it on the streets," Nick explained, "that John began taking the car out to the track." At that point, Big John figured it was time to do things right.

The National Hot Rod Association (NHRA) had established several Sports Production racing classes in 1960. The NHRA had conceived these divisions to provide sports car owners a chance to race the quarter-mile. Sports Car-Domestic class accommodated Corvettes and early Thunderbirds. Sports Car-Imported was set up for Porsches, Volkswagens, and others interested in head-to-head competition. The NHRA combined these into a single group of five Sports Production classes based on a ratio of shipping weight to advertised horsepower. Cars ran in what was called the Street Eliminator Division. Any modification, such as installing an American V-8 into a Jaguar or some such exchange, advanced the car into one of the four Modified Sports Production Classes.

For 1961, the NHRA inaugurated the "Winternationals," a series of races launched in January to begin the season at Pomona Fair Grounds. The NHRA and the chief of police of Pomona established the track and encouraged the races as a way of getting racers off the streets.

Siroonian had enough nighttime seat-time in the Corvette that Big John let the younger, lighter man carry on. It was a wise choice: Together they won the A-Sports (A/SP) class with their well-tuned 283, turning 109.96 miles per hour. During the summer, they replaced the Corvette's stock fuel injection with a Hilborn two-port injector system and a GMC 4-71 supercharger. That was good enough to give them the C-Modified Sports (CM/SP) title at the January 1962 Winternationals, winning at 113.84 miles per hour in a 12:11 elapsed time. At the Fontana, California, American Hot Rod Association (AHRA) nationals, Siroonian ran John's car to 116.84 miles per hour in an elapsed time of 12:34, to claim "Best Speed Blown."

The large tachometer obscures the small factory issue and nearly blocks the view of the speedometer—unimportant in a drag racer anyway. The view past the GMC supercharger is a challenge.

Mazmanian had legendary Southern California car painter "Junior" Conway lay on 24 hand-rubbed coats of Candy Persimmon mixed with gold leaf to get the sparkle he wanted. Between races, while competitors were retuning their engines, Big John's crew was washing and polishing his car.

But John was not just about the "go." He took pride in how his vehicles looked and his attention to detail. He hired "Junior" Conway to give the car its deep lustrous Candy Persimmon paint (24 hand-rubbed coats), brought in Eddie Martinez for the tuck-and-roll interior (even in the trunk), and chromed (or hand polished, in the case of the American Racing magnesium wheels) everything he and his crew could get to. All this effort earned him third place at the Winternationals Car Show after having won his class on the quarter-mile strip.

"Most racers at the time," Nick Mazmanian said, "used one color or even just primer for their cars . . . so if your car blew up, at least you didn't lose that much on the deal. This thought process did not extend to John. The cars were painted Candy Apple Red with 24-karat gold leaf mixed in so the colors really popped when the sun hit them. During meets, when most of the other crews were busy re-tuning and balancing the engines, John's crew was doing the same—while also washing the car. They did that between every run."

The car remained a work in progress throughout 1962, as Big John continued to revise and improve it. He took time out for magazine appearances in *Rod & Custom* (October 1962), *Hot Rod* (March 1963), and *Popular Hot Rodding* in June 1963 and again in November. Two of the magazines used on their covers an action shot of the Corvette with its Deist parachute filled and trailing behind the car.

By the time *Rod & Custom* did their typically thorough "Rod Test," John had gotten some help from legendary race engine builder Earl Wade. "At the heart of the matter," the uncredited author wrote, "the original 283-inch mill was bored to 316 cubes, with all the usual balancing and head work. A wicked Iskenderian 'Polydyne 505' camshaft, along with Isky valve springs, lifters, pushrods, etc, add to the rumble. Cragar supplied the intake, Joe Hunt the Vertex mag[neto], Jardine the headers, Hayes the clutch and flywheel—and these are only part of the goodies," the writer continued. "The car has a four-speed gearbox, to which Mazmanian added Getz gears—but even so

Before beginning the modifications to race it, *John showed it and won repeatedly at car shows throughout southern California. Once he began competing, he still maintained show-quality finish over the entire car. Courtesy Nick Mazmanian*

Rod & Custom *magazine did their typically thorough "Rod Test" on Mazmanian's car. In the story, driver Rich Siroonian admitted he always started races in second gear because the rear end was hard to control with the enormous power. Courtesy Nick Mazmanian*

Richard Siroonian never uses low, always starts in second. There's so much power that the throttle has to be treated with an extremely light touch, else the rear fishtails completely out of control."

How much power was there? Mazmanian estimated output at 600 horsepower. For *Rod & Custom*'s test, they recorded 0–60 mile-per-hour times at 4.25 seconds (with a driver and tester on board). Then, just as Siroonian did the following January to win CM/SP honors again, the young driver launched through the quarter-mile in 11.10 seconds at 129.93 miles per hour.

A chance to run Dragmaster 10.00x16 slicks at San Gabriel Dragstrip set Big John's crew, Dick Bourgeois, and engine builder Earl Wade to work with a hack saw, opening up the wheel wells. It was a "temporary fix" to the bodywork after stiffening and improving the rear suspension that became as much a part of the car's signature as its spit-shined appearance. And that only encouraged more work under the hood.

Sometime between mid-1962 and the Winternationals in January 1963, Big John replaced the bored-out 316 with a 327 that another race engine legend, Bob "Bones" Balogh, had enlarged to 338 cubic inches. They topped the engine with a GMC 6-71 supercharger and Hilborn four-port injection. This advanced them to B-Modified (BM/SP) class, where they proceeded to clean up,

running 130 miles per hour in 10.90 seconds elapsed time with "Bones" driving.

During this same work period, Mazmanian removed the factory fuel tank and installed the Moon tank in the grille (which he also had polished). He created yet another cut-out hood for the larger blower.

Records for the car indicate that of 10,939 Corvettes produced, Mazmanian grabbed the 93rd manufactured. He paid $3,934 for the car, including its optional removable hard top. His team mechanic Dick Bourgeois confided to *Rod & Custom* magazine writer that Mazmanian had $10,000 invested.

"John himself admits to $6,300," the magazine author wrote. "So the question arises: Why build a track machine that's good only for quarter-mile drags when John could have the fun of driving this car anywhere for half the expense . . .?

"First, it's a hobby with Mazmanian—he likes the sport and likes to see it grow. He enjoys improving the breed. The money isn't so important as the satisfaction of knowing he has an untouchable Corvette." And, Big John had an ambition to do the same thing with a 1963 Sting Ray.

But life had its ways of intruding on dreams. In late 1962, by the time Sting Rays were available, Rich Siroonian was in the U.S. Army. Big John had friends

Hilborn fuel injectors fed the large blower on top of a later 327-cubic-inch V-8, which Mazmanian had bored out to 338. Mazmanian conservatively estimated output at 600 horsepower.

in racing, guys named George Montgomery, Fred Stone, and others, competing in "gassers," the gasoline-fueled racers like his Corvette. But once a winner, always a competitor. For Mazmanian the next step was not another Corvette but something wilder. He built a supercharged Hemi-engined Willys.

Historians of drag racing attribute to Big John Mazmanian the distinction of being "the first current-model stock-body car to be supercharged." Within a year after John stopped racing the Corvette, Dodge and Mercury both supercharged factory-supported late-model coupes in their own efforts to promote their products. As one observer with a long view wrote, "these exhibition machines, in turn, bred a new form of late-model drag racing, one that ended up being called 'funny car.' Because of its unique position in racing history, this car may indeed be one of the true catalysts of that era."

Soon after Big John decided to challenge the other gassers, his Corvette moved on to Minnesota and raced

just briefly. It moved from owner to owner, racer to racer, and landed with a collector named John Lange. Eventually, after several years of courtship and pursuit, Minnesota collector Steve Hendrickson purchased the car from Lange in 1989 and began a complete restoration. His attention to detail extended so far as to replace the oak blocks that Big John and his crew had installed to raise the center cross member high enough for drag strip clearance, a trick that gave the car its aggressive stance and better weight transfer. Almost a decade later, in 1998, Hendrickson got the car to the Bakersfield, California, Hot Rod Reunion, where the NHRA honored Mazmanian and Big John saw his old Corvette for the first time since he sold it in 1964. In 2009, Big John Mazmanian's Candy Persimmon BM/SP "gasser" 1961 Corvette—the subject of this chapter—joined an important collection of other 1960s-era drag racers at Kuck Motorsports in Lincoln, Nebraska.

1963
CORVETTE STING RAY Z06

BATTLE GROUND

Zora Duntov could not have been a happy man during the early 1960s. His reason for living, automobile racing, had effectively been banned within General Motors by an outside organization running scared from federal interlopers. There were other ways to skin a cat, but the best of those already had been claimed. Chevy's Vince Piggins moved within the NASCAR crowds and got them cars, engines, and parts that put production-derived Chevrolet two-door coupes across the finish line first. Frank Winchell, Duntov's colleague and rival within R&D, had claimed Jim Hall and his sports racing prototype Chaparrals as his turf, and the marriage between Detroit and Texas engineering expertise created cutting-edge technology and more winner's circle appearances.

That left Duntov with production sports car racing. It was not a bad universe in which to operate in those days. Interest among competitors and spectators had grown. But it meant that in major international races, Duntov's cars might win their class but Winchell's liaison took overall honors. Duntov had ambition and he still had dreams. But he didn't have clout.

Influence and effectiveness was what Bill Mitchell and GM's design staff was all about. Hand-picked by Harley Earl to succeed him as vice president of design on December 1, 1958, Mitchell learned everything he knew from his newly-retired boss. The biggest lesson he learned was that his department had produced many successful automobiles for every division for decades.

He learned from Earl that design directed the corporation.

While the "Q" Corvette had originated as an engineering concept, a front-engine Corvette with a rear-mounted transmission, it quickly became a Design project. Mitchell assigned his favorites, Chuck Pohlmann, Tony Lapine, Peter Brock, and Bob Veryzer, to take a stab at styling a new car based on a speed-record Abarth that Mitchell had seen at the 1957 Turin auto show. He brought back a photo of the car and showed everyone, telling them this was what he wanted. The new Corvette would be a closed car as well as an open one. When management killed the Q for budgetary considerations, everyone slid their concept drawings and sketches into desk drawers.

Mitchell resurrected the idea in 1959, when he was able to acquire the 1957 Corvette SS mule car from Ed Cole. While the corporation could not race, it was unable to stop its highly visible design director from creating a new body based on the Q for his own racer. Larry Shinoda's evolutionary design was startling; Pohlmann and Brock had developed the most provocative concepts and Shinoda spun a racing roadster, dubbed the Sting Ray, off their work. Mitchell used the racer to test public reaction to such a radical new motif. If anything, however, the car was more sensitive aerodynamically than the SS had been, suffering from more severe lift as well as from the insufficient brakes and poor cooling that had plagued

Despite the AAMA recommendation against motorsports promotion, Ed Cole approved a "customer racing package," for the new Sting Ray. This car and three others introduced the package to the racing world at Riverside International Raceway in October 1962.

the SS. For Duntov, this was a nightmare. He had ideas to fix the mule's problems, but now it was Mitchell's car with a new body and he had no connection, no clout.

For Duntov, it got worse. Mitchell's talented crew (that regularly included designers Shinoda and Lapine) turned the re-bodied mule into a reliable car. Dick Thompson mastered the car's touchy handling, bringing him the C-Modified national championship for 1959. Spectators saw the car and voiced their thunderous support along the fence lines at racetracks across the country. Mitchell set Shinoda to work adapting the racer to street production. To Duntov's immense frustration, the second-generation Corvette was front-engined with a classically-proportioned long hood. And then it got even worse.

The 1957 Abarth record car—and Pohlmann's and Brock's concepts—utilized a tapered boat-tail style fastback roof line. It had a central spine that ran to the rear of the car, reminiscent of ultra-stylish French tourers of the late 1930s. It also served as an homage to Harley Earl's 1956 Golden Rocket show car. Duntov despised it. Biographer Jerry Burton surmised, "Duntov hated the split window for the same reason he hated the long hood—it obstructed the driver's view."

"No matter how wide or narrow the split, for Zora such an intrusion into the driving function was an issue worthy of war." Duntov headed to the design studio to confront the man in charge. Whether he recognized it or not, he was attempting something unprecedented in GM's history, wrestling control of a car from Design to Engineering. The last time someone other than Design had controlled the car, production engineers revised a Harley Earl Buick and the result was disaster. That was in the early 1930s. Duntov "was one man," Burton wrote, "on a limited-volume car line without a mandate from his superiors."

In the end, Duntov lost. Mitchell banned him from the Design Department. In the heat of their arguments, Mitchell even threatened to pull the independent rear suspension from the car. Whether he actually could was another question all together. He got his long hood and the 1963 Sting Ray appeared with a split rear window. Its duration may have been a compromise Ed Cole created behind the scenes; the split window became a single piece of glass from 1964 on, but that

may have been as much an economic consideration since it cost less to mold and install a single piece of glass. Jaguar's sensuous E-type had appeared a year earlier and it was beautiful. But Mitchell's Sting Ray was more: it possessed, as Harley Earl had wisely advised Mitchell, "entertainment everywhere you look around the car."

One irony after another befell the split-window coupes. In the years after Chevrolet updated the closed car with a single window, a number of owners took their cars to body shops to have a similar treatment done. As the next millennium passed, as car values escalated, original unmolested split-window Sting Rays climbed higher in resale prices.

While Duntov failed in some of his efforts with the new car, he succeeded in others that made more of a difference to aggressive drivers and racers. He raided parts bins for the full-size sedans to find dozens of front suspension pieces that improved ride, cornering, and steering feel. The rear suspension he and his engineering staff developed on CERV I yielded the geometry and many of the ideas for the Sting Ray, incorporating the half-shafts from the differential to the rear wheels as one of the active links. Jammed for space, he bolted the differential directly to the frame and installed a transverse-mounted rear leaf spring. His concept of a high roll-center, developed for the 1957 SS, reached the public with the 1963 cars. In a presentation to the Society of Automotive Engineers (SAE) in September 1962, he wrote that this configuration provided "higher resistance to roll for a given ride rate, and lower increase of possible camber," or less compromise in cornering potential.

For months after its introduction in September 1962, the car's appearance stopped viewers in their tracks and its engineering and handling attracted journalists and racers. That was another of Duntov's goals: With the AAMA recommendation still taken as the voice of law within GM, he knew it would be Chevrolet's customers who would campaign the new Corvette. He convinced Ed Cole to create a high-performance model, one fitted from the factory with stiffer springs and shocks, anti-roll bars, a limited-slip differential (Positraction), and a 36.5-gallon gas tank (the standard was 20). He developed a dual-circuit braking system

The new Special Performance Equipment option Z06 coupes were among the first 1963 Sting Rays coupes assembled in "pilot production" at St. Louis. Here, the complete rear and upper subassembly got bonded to the "birdcage." John Amgwert collection

The first of these pilot production Sting Rays went out the St. Louis assembly plant doors as racers. The "pilot" body assembly line only consisted of three stages. John Amgwert collection

and a master-cylinder and vacuum brake booster to operate them along with sintered-metallic linings for the finned drums. Engineers tweaked output of the 327-cubic-inch V-8 to achieve 360 net horsepower. Part of the package included five knock-off magnesium wheels but these did not appear for another year. Designated the Z06 option, it was an update of the earlier regular production option (RPO) 684/687 for the solid-axle cars; it cost buyers an additional $1,818.45 over the car's base price of to $4,252. Initially, Chevrolet produced the Z06 only as a coupe because there was no room in the convertible body for the larger tank. This rigid rule frustrated a number of racers, including California's Dick Guldstrand, who repeatedly had his orders for a Z06 convertible kicked back. In the spring of 1963, Chevrolet dropped the big-tank requirement and filled orders for a convertible. One went to a design staff engineer who planned to use the car to keep up with Bill Mitchell on their weekend jaunts over open roads. However, most all of the cars went to their intended audience: racers with verifiable track history.

Through September 1962, Duntov continued developing a prototype Z06 painted blue, flogging it around Daytona for hours and days. He was in a race himself against a deadline that arrived on Saturday,

October 13, in California. To reach it, he and others had to put in the miles.

The St. Louis plant practiced Sting Ray coupe production on Z06 coupes. The first of the pilot production cars went out the door as racers, some directly onto the roads, and others onto transporters. Three West Coast racers, Dave MacDonald, Jerry Grant, and Bob Bondurant, showed up at the factory doors, got a tour, picked up their cars, and followed Route 66 west toward their sponsoring dealerships for final preparations for the Los Angeles *Times* Grand Prix at Riverside International Raceway. The *Times* inaugurated a three-hour invitational event on Saturday the 13th, prior to the Grand Prix on Sunday. Bondurant drove for Washburn Chevrolet in Santa Barbara, and Dave MacDonald for Don Steves Chevrolet in Anaheim, both in California, and Grant for Alan Green Chevrolet in Seattle, Washington. Bondurant recalled the three of them had a number of impromptu races down from St. Louis before MacDonald veered off to visit relatives in Oklahoma. Their drives to the West Coast served as break-in miles for these new cars.

Another Z06 model reached California earlier, by air, treated to its flight by team owner and performance parts manufacturer Mickey Thompson, based in Long

Four new Corvettes started the Riverside race. This car wore the traditional race number California driver Dave MacDonald had adopted, 00, here in his colors with sponsorship from Don Steves Chevrolet in Anaheim, California.

Beach. One of these cars was destined for Riverside on the 13th as well, with another successful West Coast competitor, Doug Hooper, at the wheel. This was perhaps the closest of all the entries to a factory effort. Years later, Hooper recalled meeting GM president Bunkie Knudsen and being able to call Duntov directly for anything he or the team needed.

"We got everything through the back door at Chevrolet. They came with a big hauler, engines if we needed them, whatever we needed. All we had to do was call them and they'd send it."

When the car arrived nearly two months before the race, Hooper met it at Burbank Airport, about 60 miles north of Long Beach. He drove it onto Thompson's trailer and towed it to the shops. "It was really a traffic stopper. Everybody was staring at it. They had never seen a Sting Ray before."

He noticed the car had exceptionally thick fender wells, "as though it was hand made," and wires coming off the brakes where it had apparently been hooked up to some monitoring equipment."

He soon found out why Duntov's engineers paid attention to the brakes. He and Thompson's crew took it to Long Beach drag strip late one night, changed plugs, adjusted timing, and ran it hard. It hit 110 miles per hour. But when Hooper went for the brakes, "The thing went violently to the left and right. It did not brake straight. I almost hit the guard rail."

Thompson's crew worked on the brakes and tested the engine thoroughly. The high-lift cam installed in the engine caused the valve springs to bind, which would cause valves to "float," at high engine speeds because the springs could no longer react quickly enough. Valve float is fatal to engines. Thompson and Hooper set a redline "a few hundred rpms lower" for their car.

When the green flag fell on Saturday, drivers sprinted across the back straight to their cars parked diagonally, as in the Le Mans race in France. History does not record who earned the pole, but Bondurant, MacDonald, and Grant qualified near the front. Four cars separated them from Doug Hooper, who had qualified more conservatively with his lower redline. Two of those were solid axle Corvettes. The third was a Porsche. The fourth was an English sports car with a Ford V-8 called the Cobra.

A Texan with impeccable racing credentials named Carroll Shelby (he had won Le Mans in 1959 driving an Aston Martin with Roy Salvadori), had approached Chevrolet in 1959 to buy three Corvettes without their bodies. He, Chaparral founder Jim Hall, and another sports car racer named Gary Laughlin, had struck a deal with Italian body designer Sergio Scaglietti for him to fabricate three aluminum coupes to fit a Corvette chassis. The three men wanted to develop a "production" sports car for Sports Car Club of America (SCCA) races. They completed the cars though none ever raced. It was another step in Carroll Shelby's formulation. This was an idea bred from his early days racing an Allard with a Cadillac engine, that an American V-8 could power a lightweight nimble English sports car to victory. When he learned that AC Cars was losing its engine maker, he approached Chevrolet again, but this time they said no. Everyone from Bunkie Knudsen on down reckoned that they did not need a Corvette-powered lightweight sports car beating Corvettes on the track.

Shelby, who already harbored ill feelings toward Enzo Ferrari, Italy's legendary race car producer, added the Chevrolet to his list. He found a receptive ear in Ford Motor Company's head of product planning, Don Frey, when he told them that if they provided him six engines and a few dollars, he would kick Ferraris *and* Corvettes all over the racetrack. Coincidentally, the Los Angeles *Times* G.P. organizers had invited not only Chevrolet Corvettes to the race but they also had extended a welcome to Carroll Shelby.

"I knew it was going to be there," Doug Hooper recalled. "But nobody knew what to expect. It was just an AC Ace with a Ford V-8 in it. I can't really say I was concerned about that Cobra before Riverside. Not at all."

Who knew?

The statistics suggested it might be an uneven match. Corvettes, in Z06 trim including steel wheels (which were available an inch wider than the "stock" knock offs to fit SCCA rules), weighed 3,100 pounds; the Cobra was 1,000 pounds lighter. The Corvette had inadequate drum brakes; the Cobra raced with disc brakes, which allowed drivers to stay on the power deeper into corners, and its lighter weight let them accelerate out of corners faster.

The Z06 option included the 360-horsepower Rochester fuel-injected 327-cubic-inch V-8. A dual-circuit braking system (at far left) incorporated a vacuum booster and master cylinder that operated sintered-metallic brake linings inside heavily finned brake drums.

For the first hour, Dave MacDonald fought for the lead with Billy Krause in the Cobra. In racing parlance, he played the role of the rabbit, running hard and fast against the competition to force them to make a mistake or break. It worked. Just before the hour ended, MacDonald's left rear wheel separated from the car as a wheel bearing failed. A few minutes into the second hour, the same fate befell Krause's Cobra. During that hour, both Bondurant and Grant retired with blown engines—a prediction Hooper and Thompson had made before lowering their redline. The Porsche gridded a few spots ahead of Doug Hooper challenged him near the end of the third hour, but Hooper held him off and gave Mickey Thompson's car the win.

"I don't think it's ever been done before," a joyful Thompson told the gathered media, "a new production car winning the first time out!" Thompson's black car, No. 119, has disappeared. Collectors and racing historians look for it to this day. The Dave MacDonald rabbit—the subject of this chapter, wearing his traditional No. 00—is in a private collection of significant race cars of all makes in the Midwest.

Because the Z06 was meant to race in Sports Car Club of America (SCCA) production classes, the cars kept most of the production interior. Per Z06 code, the heater and radio were deleted but full instrumentation was retained.

1963
LIGHTWEIGHT GRAND SPORT COUPE

CASUALTY OF WARS

Nineteen Hundred Sixty-Two was a good year for Corvette racers. From February through September, the cars and their drivers won again and again. When Chevrolet introduced the Sting Ray Z06 at Riverside International Raceway in mid-October, Doug Hooper crossed the finish line first. But Carroll Shelby's menacing Cobra had hounded him. It was a car that surprised and then disappointed Corvette racers. The potential of this much lighter roadster—2,026 pounds compared to the Z06's 2,943—provided them a glimpse of the future. There were few podiums in sight.

Zora Duntov knew about the Cobra. But he already had moved on. Bunkie Knudsen became Chevrolet's general manager in December 1961, and he ignored the AAMA recommendation against racing. He wanted to enhance his division's reputation in every type of motor sports. In early 1962, he approved funding for Duntov's CERV II mid-engine coupe. However, the plan leaked out and the chairman exercised his power again.

Knudsen and Duntov shifted gears and strategized motor sports as a marketing tool: Could they conceive a car that looked like the new Sting Ray but had real competitive potential? It had to be much lighter and more powerful. Carroll Shelby was working toward 100 Cobras, the number the Fédération Internationale de l'Automobile (FIA) required for homologation as a "production" racer. Duntov proposed manufacturing 125 to ensure approval. Knudsen and Duntov considered a street production run of 1,000 cars or

more. Dealers would sell the cars to enthusiasts who watched the new lightweight coupes win.

Duntov's group secretly began preparing a prototype chassis for the new "Light Weight." They developed a strong, simple ladder frame with robust but thin-wall steel tubes that ran parallel from nose to tail. The front rose to accommodate suspension and steering pieces, and the rear kicked up to accept the axle and its independent suspension, carrying over a variation of the production car's transverse leaf. Engineers fitted Girling solid disc brakes at all four corners. Parallel tubes kept design and fabrication fast and simple. However, this configuration left no bulge to drop in the driver seat or passenger area. Engineers set the floor pan on top of the tubes and mounted the thin driver seat above that.

While working on the open-wheeled CERV I, Duntov developed a new engine based on the 327-cubic-inch block. Bore at 4 inches and stroke at 3.75 inches yielded 377 cubic inches total displacement. Engineers configured heads with two spark plugs per cylinder. Theoretical output reached 550 horsepower at 6,400 rpm with torque of 500 pound-feet at 5,200 rpm. They cast the new block in aluminum. When Duntov's engineers filed homologation papers for the car with the FIA, they quoted dry weight at 1,908 pounds, 1,000 less than a Z06.

Technicians in the engineer prototype shop hand-laid a fiberglass body just 0.04 inch thick. Duntov wanted owners to be able to remove the body from the chassis in one piece. Engineers abandoned the

Chevrolet general manager "Bunkie" Knudsen agreed with Zora Duntov
that motorsports was a marketing opportunity. The Fédération Internationale de
l'Automobile *(FIA)* required 100 cars for homologation, and Knudsen and Duntov both
envisioned a run of 1,000 "replicas" for series production.

"birdcage" structure that supported the production coupe's doors and roof. They used an ultra-light aluminum framework formed by hand to surround the doors and windows. They bonded it to the fiberglass.

Styling chief Bill Mitchell had barred Duntov from Styling following their battles over the production Sting Ray's long nose and its split rear window, so the finished body bore few of the changes Duntov had hoped to make. Technicians bolted it onto the chassis in seven places but it sat 2 inches higher than production cars, a fact that affected its aerodynamics.

Engineers completed GS001 on November 14, 1962. With no 377 available yet, they installed a production 327-cubic-inch, 360-horsepower engine for tests. A small badge on the rear identified it as Corvette Grand Sport.

Imprudently, Duntov and his staff took the car to Sebring for tests on December 15 and 16, 1962, to evaluate brakes, tires, and wheels. They hired veteran racers Dick Thompson and Masten Gregory for the trials. Thompson had achieved success in Corvettes by using their handling characteristics to augment the car's chronically insufficient brakes. He relied on "getting the car a little sideways" to scrub speed through faster turns to conserve his brakes for slower ones. The heft of the new Z06 allowed him to retain that technique. This was not so successful with the Grand Sport.

"If you got the Light Weight a little bit out there," he recalled in an interview in 2009, "you spun. And it would keep going around. You had to be very precise. We learned to apply the brakes earlier with a lighter touch."

Thompson and Gregory overheated the solid ½-inch-thick Girling rotors. GM-Delco-Morraine brake expert Ashod Torosian made notes. Back in Warren, engineers developed and installed internally-ventilated 1-inch-thick rotors.

Two days of testing in Florida were too public. Chairman Frederic Donner learned of Duntov's doings and Knudsen's complicity. Donner came down hard, shutting down the project on January 21, 1963. Parts had arrived for more Light Weights and engineers already had assembled the others. Duntov's aluminum 377-cubic-inch twin-plug engine, however, advanced no further than one prototype. According to Duntov biographer Jerry Burton, "Knowing he had Ed Cole's moral—if not formal—support, Duntov decided to defy

the ban," Burton wrote. "His orders from upstairs were not to build any more cars, but there was nothing said about the cars that had already been built." So Duntov loaned the Grand Sports to trusted teams who kept his secret. He chose to hide GS001 and GS002 deep in the back rooms of engineering. In February 1963, GS003 went to suburban Chicago dealer and racer Dick Doane. Car GS004, the subject of this chapter, went to Grady Davis, head of research at Gulf Oil.

Donner's January 21 memo permanently crippled the cars. With so few cars, the FIA classed the Grand Sport in C-Modified class. Instead of racing Carroll Shelby's Cobras, Grand Sports confronted sports racers like Jim Hall's Chaparrals (powered by engines from Frank Mitchell's R&D efforts).

By April, Davis was ready with GS004. Dick Thompson debuted the car at Marlboro Raceway outside Marlboro, Maryland, on April 7. A faulty fuel injector stalled him on the start. He finished last overall but he was the only car running in C-Modified at the end, so he captured the Grand Sport's first victory. Three weeks later at Virginia International Raceway in Danville, Virginia, Ed Lowther substituted for Thompson and brought GS004 home in fourth overall, third in C-Modified. Back at Marlboro in May, Thompson finished third in class, and at the June Sprints at Road America in Wisconsin, he took third overall as he prepared for Watkins Glen on August 24. As the first Grand Sport out of Chevrolet's shops, Thompson's races and Gulf's testing turned GS004 into Duntov's development mule.

"I loved that Light Weight Corvette. That's what everybody called it," Thompson recalled. "With Grady we worked hard. We gained an inch here, an inch and a little bit there . . . I came to read it very easily; I knew what it was going to do next. It didn't surprise me. After a little bit of driving, I knew when the rear end was going to break loose. That car gave you lots of signals."

One of its signals was front-end lift. Thompson had raced Bill Mitchell's Sting Ray roadster, the car built from Duntov's rebodied 1957 SS mule. Its aerodynamic strengths worked when the car was pointed straight ahead. When Thompson hung the tail out to scrub speed in the corners, airflow got cluttered. He discovered the Grand Sport's modified Sting Ray body formed an airfoil

One of Duntov's strongest arguments with Bill Mitchell about the appearance of the new Sting Ray centered on the split rear-window configuration of the production cars. For the Grand Sport racers, Duntov did away with the center divider.

whose lift tendencies were exaggerated by the slightly higher body height and the recessed radiator intake below the car's leading edge. It came clear in late July at Meadowdale, a hilly circuit northwest of Chicago.

"I went over the top of a hill," he recalled, "and the nose lifted up. I went along on the rear wheels a long way down that hill. When the front end came down, it smashed part of the front suspension. I went on, and I finished the race. But I didn't worry too much about handling for the rest of the race. There was none."

This was the era before rear wings and chin spoilers to correct such problems. Mechanics worked to improve cornering and power. After Meadowdale, Davis' engineers installed a new twin-air meter Rochester fuel injection that pumped 1,100 cubic feet per minute of air into the engine. They added a mailbox-sized air scoop to the hood over the inlets to evacuate air from under the hood and lessen the front lift tendencies. At Connellsville Airport in Pennsylvania, an SCCA

regional in mid-August, Davis' work paid off. Thompson won outright with GS004.

"My favorite race of all in the Light Weight was at Watkins Glen [August 25, 1963]. That track has slow turns, fast turns, really fast turns, some good long straights. I had a really good time there. I qualified well. At the start, my best friend, Walt Hansgen was beside me in a Maserati. Behind me was Augie Pabst in a Ferrari. And I managed to beat them. I knew they were friends of mine so they wouldn't pull any nasty stuff." Harry Heuer in his potent Chaparral stayed with Thompson until lap 17, when Heuer got around Thompson in traffic. Thompson pressed Heuer hard and 10 laps later, Heuer's rear end failed in a cloud of smoke. Thompson shot past and led until the end.

"The Light Weight was fast enough to scare most every driver. It was just insanely fast." Thompson and Grady Davis finished the season in fourth place in C/Modified. Then Duntov called his children home.

Winchell still was head of R&D and Jim Musser was his lieutenant, working on tires, wheels, and suspensions. Duntov loaned them GS005. Winchell invited in Roger Penske, a successful racer who was a sales engineer with Alcoa Aluminum, to consult with Chevrolet R&D as they considered casting engine blocks and other parts in aluminum. Winchell, Musser, and Penske took the car to nearby Waterford Hills to test. Over the course of dozens of laps, tire and wheel widths grew from 6 inches to 9s and 11s. This raised skid pad capability from 0.9g up to 1.1g. It was the beginning of a long relationship with Penske.

In October, engineers fitted new rear fender flares to accommodate the wider tires. They added air vents along the rear filler panel to improve rear brake and differential cooling, and they opened side air scoops to enhance front brake and engine ventilation.

According to Paul van Valkenburgh in *Chevrolet = Racing . . .?*, Duntov's 377-cubic-inch, dual-overhead cam engine wasn't finished and dynamometer-tested until GS003 and GS004 were out the door. After it was ready, he held it up; getting the engine to Grady Davis might alert GM's front office. His subterfuge worked; in November 1963, the cars were back and no one had heard from Chairman Donner. There was one more chance to show the racing world what Grand Sports could do: Nassau Speed Weeks, from December 1 through 8, 1963. Duntov's engineers installed the anxiously awaited aluminum 377 V-8 engines with four 58mm DCOE Weber side draft carburetors. This combination developed 485 horsepower at 6,000 rpm. Duntov needed another outsider to race the cars.

That outsider was 23-year-old John Mecom, a Texas oil heir who had not yet inherited responsibility in his family's empire. In mid-1962, he founded Mecom Racing, hiring Penske, Augie Pabst, and A. J. Foyt as his drivers. His purchases favored mid-engine sports racers but he accepted Duntov's offer to run the Light Weights, GS003, GS004, and GS005. The three cars, painted in Mecom's team colors, Cadillac's Pelham Blue, joined his Lola GT, Cooper, and Scarab. It was total performance, powered by Chevrolet.

The "Bahamas Speed Weeks" surrounded five nights of parties with two weekends of racing. To encourage participation, founder Sherman "Red" Crise

and the tourism board had extended 50 expenses-paid invitations (and dozens of un-reimbursed offers) each year since 1954. Crise often amended FIA regulations to suit tourist interests. For 1963, he declared that prototypes (Corvette Grand Sports) would run in the same events (but in separate classes) as Shelby Cobra grand touring production cars.

The S.S. *Bahama Star* nuzzled the docks at the Port of Nassau on November 30, 1963, a day before racing began. Mecom and his drivers joined Carroll Shelby and his Cobra team waiting for cars to be unloaded. The pale blue Grand Sports floated off the ship, suspended in their slings. Shelby, his head engineer Phil Remington, and his chief driver Ken Miles did everything but pry the Light Weights apart to see what lurked under their hoods. Pictures of the day made by Shelby's staff photographer Dave Friedman showed Carroll looking concerned. A number of Chevrolet engineers showed up in Friedman's pictures, men who coincidentally chose to take their annual vacations in Nassau that week. Among them was Zora Duntov.

The Grand Sports got off to a slow start at Nassau. None did well the first day and Roger Penske, who had practiced in GS004, heard expensive noises coming from his engine. He withdrew. Overheated differentials sidelined the other cars throughout the day. Outside providers had improperly adjusted and insufficiently broken in the rear-end gear sets. Inadequate cooling cooked them. In addition, drivers had experienced fuel starvation in hard cornering and severe front end lift at high speeds.

On Tuesday, another GM engineer suddenly needed a vacation in Nassau. His bags included several properly broken-in differential gear sets. Already on "vacation," Chevrolet engineer Gib Hufstader reconfigured Chevrolet passenger car transmission radiators to cool differential oil. He mounted them under small shrouds outside of the body behind the rear window. Adjusting floats in the Weber carburetors tamed some fuel feed problems but the body presented aerodynamics dilemmas engineers never could solve.

During Friday's 25-lap Governor's race, Penske finished third overall, first in prototype class in GS004. The nearest Cobras placed eleventh and twelfth overall. Sunday's 56-lap main event was more of the same with

Engineers adopted the stock instrument panel but fabricated it in lightweight plastic instead of diecast metal. The speedometer reads up to 200 miles per hour.

Dick Thompson crossing the line fourth in GS004. On the high speed stretches of Nassau's Oakes Circuit, air pressure under the hoods of the Grand Sports broke tie-downs and required repeated pit stops for crews to racer-tape the hoods down on GS003 and GS004. This cost Thompson and teammate John Cannon better finishes. The following morning, with the season finally over, John Mecom offered French motoring journalist Bernard Cahier one of the Grand Sports for a story.

"Gone was the docile Corvette;" he wrote in the March 1964 issue of *Sports Car Graphic*, "the lamb turned quickly into a tiger and I was breathless with the stupendous acceleration of the car. With 480 horsepower for a weight of 2,000 pounds . . . I was concentrating mainly on applying the right amount of power not to spin the wheels wildly or come out of corners sideways. . . . If you really want to show off you can leave rubber marks for a quarter of a mile, as you still get wheel spin when putting it into third gear."

Back in Michigan, Duntov responded immediately to the performance in Nassau. In a memo to Jim Premo of R&D, unearthed by Duntov biographer Jerry Burton, Duntov alternated between boasting and boosterism, celebrating "the superiority of Light Corvettes over

Ford Cobras and all other GT and GT prototypes." Race results had appeared in newspapers, yet no new recriminations rained down from the chairman's office. Duntov felt encouraged to move ahead toward Daytona, Sebring, and perhaps even Le Mans.

The large frontal area of the Light Weights made it hard to reach peak speeds at Daytona and Le Mans. Tests and data analyses suggested to Duntov that the cars could run faster without tops. In January 1964, Tech Center staff sliced the roofs off GS001 and GS002, cars Duntov had kept hidden for more than a year. Technicians fitted low windscreens and headrest fairings. They enclosed a roll bar in a fiberglass hoop behind the cockpit.

Mecom Racing cars returned to engineering for the next round of updates. Higher-rate springs and new hood ventilation aimed at further reducing air pressure under the hood were on the menu.

Then Donner spoke, summoning Knudsen to tell Duntov he no longer could associate with Mecom. Knudsen and Ed Cole had absorbed the brunt of Donner's frustration with Duntov. Still, Donner commanded Knudsen to "dispose" of all the cars, ordering them burnt to the ground.

Duntov developed an aluminum-block 377-cubic-inch V-8 for CERV I, his open-wheel prototype. With the potential of 550 horsepower, he adopted it for the new lightweight Grand Sport.

(During the 2003 50th Anniversary year, a man approached Dick Guldstrand and introduced himself as a GM retiree. He had the assignment to destroy the Grand Sports. He claimed he destroyed the sixth Grand Sport and, in front of the witness who photographed it, he completely destroyed it. "He told me when he finished," Guldstrand reported in late 2009, "the witness agreed he proved he knew how to do it. The man said he'd take care of the rest but he didn't have time right then. They agreed he would destroy the remaining cars later. He, Duntov, and others hurriedly moved the remaining two roadsters and three coupes around to the large storage facility below the Styling Center auditorium.")

Engineers replaced engines in the surviving coupes, substituting cast-iron 377 blocks for the aluminum from Nassau. Defying Donner's orders, a transporter headed back to Houston to Mecom's shops along with an invoice for all the roadsters and coupes. However, when the transporter reached Houston, only three coupes were on board. The roadsters, while legally Mecom's cars, remained hidden in Warren, Michigan. John sold and shipped GS005 to Jim Hall, who promptly sent it to Roger Penske to prepare it for the 1964 season. Mecom kept coupes GS003 and GS004 in his shops, holding on to GS003 to prep it for Sebring. He had hired Dallas racer and Chevrolet dealer Delmo Johnson to campaign GS004 locally.

"At that time, to get a bigger crowd for Sunday sports car races," Delmo Johnson recalled in an interview late in 2009, "we staged funny things like fights on the grid, personal grudges against each other for the fun of it. It excited people and they came out to see me and Jim Hall have a fight, or me and Carroll Shelby square off."

In 1964, the SCCA held its national convention in Dallas and scheduled a weekend of racing at nearby Green Valley Raceway. Shelby had promised to run an A-production Cobra and the Cobra-powered tube-frame Cooper called the King Cobra. To promote a crowd, Delmo announced he would enter Mecom's GS004 in A-Production as a "Racing Sting Ray."

"Shelby and I were both interviewed by the local newspaper," Johnson explained. "He was sitting at one desk and I was at another and we were laughing at each other's answers. The interviewer would ask me a question and Shelby would answer it, and vice versa." Practice Saturday frustrated Delmo.

"John [Mecom] was the nicest man in the world," Johnson recalled in an interview in 2009, "but he couldn't drive anything but automatic transmissions. He'd been driving the Grand Sport [No. 004] around the airport in Houston and it didn't help the clutch any."

Johnson's mechanics worked Saturday to get the clutch working. Sunday saw 12,000 people in the stands to watch a two-race grudge match unfold. At the last minute, to elevate the drama, Shelby withdrew his A-Production Cobra, leaving Johnson to battle the low-slung mid-engine King Cobra.

"Long story short, the car didn't perform well. I managed to stay on the same lap but just barely. But it was a fun race and the local club made a lot of money out if it."

Within weeks, Mecom shipped GS004 to Grady Davis at Gulf. Don Yenko stepped in for Dick Thompson at the United States Road Race of Champions (USRRC) season opener on March 1, 1964, at Augusta International Speedway. Yenko finished 14th overall. Immediately after that race, and with other plans set for the remainder of the year, Davis wanted to return the car to Duntov. Duntov knew Johnson and offered him GS004 for $4,000. Johnson jumped on it and put his mechanics to work preparing the car to join Mecom and Jim Hall/Roger Penske at Sebring.

Once there, Johnson and co-driver Dave Morgan qualified in twelfth. They used the Grand Sport's immense power and torque on the long straights but gave away positions through the corners. The best finish went to Penske and Hall, 18th overall and fourth in prototype GT class. Ferraris and Cobras claimed the first eight spots. Johnson's and Morgan's weekend started bad and got worse. A practice session crash severely damaged the rear end of the car, nearly separating the gas tank from the racer. At the start, Johnson recalled, "the back end of the car was mostly painted racer tape." But challenges continued with little problems slowing their pace. At one point, the gas pedal linkage separated from the carburetors. Johnson sized up the problem, removed a lace from one of his shoes, and limped the car back to the pits. Still running at the race's end, they completed 144 laps, some 70 fewer than the winning Ferrari.

Through much of the rest of 1964, Mecom's GS003 and Jim Hall's GS005 lapsed into semi-retirement. Only Johnson continued a vigorous campaign, racing nearly every weekend at local and regional contests throughout the south. One particularly memorable competition arrived late in 1964 when the Mexican government staged an event they called *Carrera de Costa a Costa*, the race from coast to coast.

"The race went from Vera Cruz to Mexico City," Johnson explained, "stopped overnight, and then continued on down to Acapulco the next day. My mechanics did several conversions on the car. We replaced the factory gas tank with one that held fifty-five gallons. At speed that car was getting only about two miles a gallon."

Johnson trucked the car to Mexico City and with a translator from his sponsoring company riding along, they set off to Vera Cruz so Johnson could run in the new engine. There were incidents—at around 150 miles per hour, they passed local police . . . who waved. An off-road excursion peeled off the oil filter, so they bought one off the engine of a passing Chevrolet taxi. A rear differential-cooler line separated and gears seized just outside of Vera Cruz. Johnson and his translator abandoned the car and walked to the first cantina they encountered to wait for his support truck. His mechanic, Bill Goodfellow, found them by looking for the bar nearest to the car.

It was a wide-open race; the only rule seemed to be that there were no rules. "We drove through the country as fast as we could go." Johnson said. "We wouldn't get a speeding ticket. We had government permission.

"We went through towns where you couldn't see the road for all the people standing there. We all were going one hundred-fifty, one hundred-sixty miles an hour just a few feet from them. The route went through one town that had a series of bumps in the road. I couldn't see the bumps for all the people. I hit this series of dips and the car went airborne. When it came back down I was, oh, maybe thirty degrees from going straight. So it took about a zig-zag-zig-zag to correct it. By the time I got it straight, all the people were gone.

I don't know where they went; I was on the right road, but all the sudden I had a clear path in front of me."

Johnson crossed the line in second overall. However, since he was not Mexican, the organizers disqualified him. They paid prize money to the first ten places. (He did get the second place trophy, though.)

Both Johnson and Roger Penske retired at the end of the 1964 season. Like Penske, business pressures called Johnson away from sport.

"When I quit racing," Johnson recalled, "I kept the Grand Sport. I was going to rebuild it. During the Mexican road race, I hit bottom so many times, the frame had dragged so many times, I had broken all the shock mounts."

Barely three years old, the Grand Sports were old technology, drifting into retirement and obscurity. They exemplified the best of the previous generation of race cars. Even front-engine Cobras could only chase mid-engine racers. Motor sports journalist Bill Oursler interviewed Duntov several years after his retirement in 1975. The engineer was hard on himself and on the Grand Sports.

"It was a quick and dirty sledgehammer project that we put together in a couple of months," he told Oursler. "There were so many compromises and so many constraints that we made something of which I am not particularly proud."

Delmo Johnson disagreed.

"I drove my car probably thirty thousand miles," Johnson recalled recently, referring to GS004, the subject of this chapter. "All those other drivers, they've got races and hours in their cars. I've got *days* in mine. Remember, I ran my Grand Sport for two years racing more than forty weekends each year. I really got to know it.

"The best part of that car, well, it always was a 'modified' car so we could put any engine configuration we wanted to in it. We always had big powerful engines.

"The worst part was the front end wouldn't stay on the ground. It kind of bounced. Every time you hit the ground you had to make sure the wheels were straight.

"I loved that car," Johnson explained. "It did everything it was supposed to do for me. It won a lot of races. Zora [Duntov] went through a lot to build that car. He almost got fired twice for it. I think it was probably Zora's crown jewel."

At the end of the 1963 season, Duntov called in all his Grand Sport loans but then sent one to Chevrolet research and development (R&D) for tire and wheel testing at nearby Waterford Hills. A day of work expanded wheel widths from 6-inch front and rear, to 9-inch fronts and 11-inch rears.

1964
CERV II

RACING UNDER THE RADAR

Zora Duntov wanted to win Le Mans. Not just a class victory but First Place. Overall. The fastest, fleetest, strongest survivor still standing after 24 hours.

The under-developed SS of 1957 had provided him notebooks full of lessons about components, engineering, development, and testing. The 1959 Sting Ray racer that Bill Mitchell developed from the SS mule added more bulk and data to his knowledge of aerodynamics, and of race preparation and strategy. Between CERV I and the Cunningham effort at Le Mans in 1960, he developed theories about tire technology, race car handling, and drive systems. A 24-hour victory was impossible without attention to all of these areas.

In his mind he began to conceive his Le Mans racer. He had seen Chevrolet race engines go the distance, 12 hours at Sebring, 24 in France. This encouraged him. But those were only class victories. He needed more power, he knew, enough power—500 horsepower, perhaps 550—to run consistently, reliably, and without drama in the lead or near it through 24 hours. Tire technology barely had kept up with the CERV I output at 500 horses. Duntov came to believe that driving four wheels gave him a better chance of controlling additional power.

Where he had conceived CERV I with Indianapolis in mind, those rules called for open wheels. Le Mans regulations required that builders enclose wheels and tires within the bodywork. Duntov's friendship with Tony Lapine had developed when they worked on

the SS, and his relationship with Larry Shinoda had solidified as they worked together on CERV I. Duntov went back to Tony and Larry and asked them to think about a sports racing design. They developed both a coupe and a roadster. He sent a memo to Chevrolet's chief engineer Harry Barr on January 3, 1962. In this proposal, according to Duntov biographer Jerry Burton, Zora "suggested the use of such a car in world championship endurance events, such as Le Mans and Sebring, which were open to prototype and experimental cars" with displacement limited to 240 cubic inches. He proposed constructing a 1,500-pound open cockpit racer using an aluminum-block Chevy V-8 that would develop 400 horsepower. Duntov's engineers produced plans that, according to Burton, "included a manually controlled power-shifted transmission and an engine featuring three-valve heads."

It was not to be. Vince Piggins supported NASCAR teams and Frank Winchell was working with Texan Jim Hall on his Chaparral project. These were projects far outside the company walls. Duntov's undisguised race car was too obvious even as a secret project. Disappointed but not dissuaded, he set the idea aside and turned to making a more aggressive Sting Ray, a car he called the Light Weight Corvette, the Grand Sport.

After GM had promoted Ed Cole to head the car and truck group in 1961, Semon E. "Bunkie" Knudsen stepped up as general manager of Chevrolet. Knudsen's father had been GM president in the 1940s and when

Duntov, already an outspoken and controversial engineer, had to compete with other engineering project heads who were more shrewd and circumspect in their dealings with upper management. Duntov was constantly fighting for money to fund his projects.

In early 1962, Zora Duntov proposed a car like this to chief engineer Harry Barr, as the kind of vehicle Chevrolet could use to compete at international endurance races, such as Le Mans and Sebring. His concept was a 1,500-pound open car with 400 horsepower.

Bunkie asked for a car as a teenager, his father gave him one, in pieces, challenging the young man to put it together. Performance became a driving force in the younger Knudsen's career, aiding and encouraging Pontiac participation in NASCAR despite the AAMA "recommendation" against it. With Knudsen, Duntov had as strong ally in the front office than he'd had with Ed Cole.

In 1962, Ford Motor Company turned its back on the AAMA, launching a new marketing plan called "Total Performance Powered by Ford." Ford had attempted to acquire Ferrari the next year, but the canny Italian race car maker used the negotiations to pressure Fiat and the Italian government into a purchase instead. That unleashed the full fury of Henry Ford's rage and within months he launched an international racing program with Le Mans as the bulls-eye and Enzo Ferrari in the center of the cross-hairs. Duntov, chastened by what Ford-powered Shelby Cobras did to his Sting Ray racers, set Ford as his target.

Duntov studied four-wheel-drive racers from Germany between the wars; he developed his own theories about how to master the complexities of weight and power transfer to all four tires so the car was stable in acceleration, braking, and maneuvering. He settled on employing a transmission and torque converter for each end of the car, "reasoning," as biographer Jerry Burton wrote, "that a pair of transmissions would be lighter than one large transmission plus clutch, transfer case and drive shaft. It was an all-new principle, and Duntov earned a patent on it."

To tame the vehicle and traction dynamics from full acceleration through to full braking, he adopted new lightweight two-speed transaxles that Frank Winchell's engineers were developing for the Chaparral. Paul Van Valkenburgh, an engineer working for Winchell at the time, wrote about the project in his book *Chevrolet = Racing . . .?*

"For the torque split that Duntov thought was proper, he called upon the converter engineers to design the front and rear with different torque ratios at the same rpm." This concept utilized weight transfer to shift more engine torque to the rear wheels under acceleration and then nearly balance it front-to-rear at high speed.

Duntov relied on the same 377-cubic-inch all-aluminum engine he had used in CERV I (and the Grand Sports), complete with its Hilborn fuel injection. At the Milford Proving Ground large circle, he accelerated from 0 to 60 miles per hour in 2.8

Wind tunnel tests of the sleek body that stylists Tony Lapine and Larry Shinoda developed failed to reveal lifting forces. To keep the car on the ground, Duntov and his engineers developed a retractable rear spoiler they nicknamed "the cow tongue."

seconds and bettered CERV I's lap speed, reaching 214.01 miles per hour on wide (for the era) Firestone 9.5x15 tires on all four wheels. He and his staff assembled the new Lapine-Shinoda roadster body for development, holding the coupe configuration as part of their strategy for Le Mans. Wind tunnel testing gave the designers a sleek body form. Once again, however, the emerging science of aerodynamics and automotive lift were less clear in the tunnel. On the track, Duntov related to Jerry Burton, "lifting forces were so high, I felt like I was in a wheelbarrow and a giant hand picked me up at one-hundred fifty miles per hour." To keep the car on the ground, he and his engineers developed a retractable blade spoiler they nicknamed "the cow tongue."

Keeping the car on the ground, developing the power, taming the handling, reaching 214 miles per hour—those were the easy challenges. Funding the car was the real trial that Duntov and CERV II faced. Though he still worked for R&D, he devoted much of his time to Corvette racing developments. Vince Piggins, who managed "special projects," expended his efforts "managing" NASCAR support. Duntov's fellow senior engineer in R&D, Frank Winchell, was updating the Corvair and worked through the backdoor to get

engines and transmissions to Chaparral. With all other things being equal and with only so much "research and development" money available, allocations often went to the man who best played the corporate games. "Winchell may have been a better fit in a large corporation like GM," Jerry Burton wrote. "While extremely competitive, he didn't mind keeping a low profile, as opposed to Duntov, who enjoyed basking in the limelight even if it meant irritating senior GM managers like Ed Cole."

Winchell's programs naturally got large sums of money because of their production applications, a reality that Duntov recognized but may have chaffed at. As Jerry Burton surmised, "For the key decision-makers in the corporation, directing more money into Winchell's programs was their way of controlling Duntov's zeal for high-profile activities. . . . If GM was going to go racing, they much preferred to fly under the radar with Winchell and Chaparral." Duntov may have been his own best public relations agency but he often was his own worst enemy.

With Jim Hall's help, Chaparral and Winchell developed a car they called GS2, or Grand Sport 2. Engineer/historian Van Valkenburgh theorized that Winchell may have felt the need to take the Grand

Other engineers within Chevrolet supported Chaparral-owner Jim Hall's efforts at endurance racing, and in tests CERV II fell behind the Chaparral in performance and handling. In March 1964, Duntov learned Chevrolet would support the Chaparrals at Le Mans, and his project was dead.

The all-aluminum 377-cubic-inch V-8 provided the lightweight roadster with astonishing performance. At Milford Proving Ground, acceleration tests revealed 0- to 60-mile-per-hour times at 2.8 seconds.

Sport, Duntov's "baby," down a notch. The GS2 was a rear-wheel-drive version of Duntov's CERV II, using an automatic transmission that Frank Winchell had designed. The GS2 went to Hall's Midland, Texas, development facility and test track, Rattlesnake Raceway. Soon it became apparent that Duntov's CERV II had to go as well for comparison purposes.

In March 1964, Duntov watched in disappointment as front transaxle problems and other glitches with the disc brakes left CERV II in the dust behind the GS2. A few months later, his champion, Bunkie Knudsen clipped the wings of CERV II permanently in an internal memo announcing that Chaparral would carry Chevrolet's banner at Le Mans. CERV II went into storage.

In 1968, Duntov and CERV II got a rematch against an updated GS2B for tire evaluations. The Winchell/Chaparral machine had adopted four-wheel drive as part of its test to compare its traction and handling against Jim Hall's revolutionary 2J, which used

motorized fans at the rear. The so-called "sucker car" relied on air forcibly evacuated from underneath the car to hold it tightly to the road surface.

Duntov mounted an aluminum 427-cubic-inch displacement engine, the ZL1 engine, in CERV II. The GS2B ran with a 327. With the smaller engine, the R&D car weighed considerably less. Winchell's GS2B ran away from the CERV II again.

It marked the end of an idea and a turning point in its developer's career. This was the closest any pure-bred Duntov concept ever got to a racetrack. Soon afterward, the car that is the subject of this chapter joined its open-wheeled sibling in storage. In 1971, General Motors donated both of them to Briggs Cunningham's museum in Costa Mesa, California. Cunningham closed down his museum in 1987 and sold his collection to Florida's Miles Collier. Soon after, Collier sold both cars to collectors Steve Hendrickson and K. D. James. About a decade ago, CERV II joined a private collection in Ohio, where it remains today.

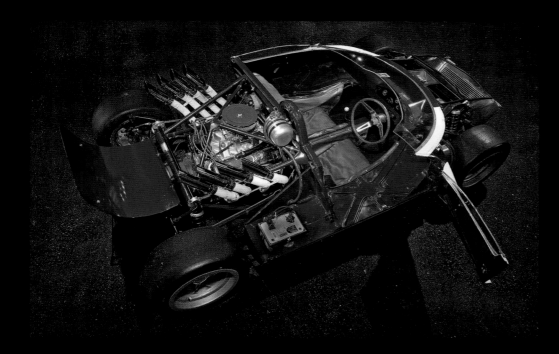

Later in its career, the roadster swapped out the aluminum 377 for an aluminum-block ZL1 427-cubic-inch engine. Even with all-wheel-drive, handling 600 horsepower was a challenge.

With the handling and traction problems his lightweight CERV I open-wheeler had endured, Duntov concluded all-wheel-drive would better handle powerful engines and cornering forces.

1966

L88 COUPE

YOU NEVER CHEAT UNTIL YOU'RE CAUGHT

Roger Penske had wrestled with a dilemma. Off the racetrack, he worked as a sales engineer for Alcoa Aluminum. He had graduated from Lehigh University in 1959 with a business degree specializing in industrial management. He was as good at engineering as he was at driving race cars. His success during the 1964 Bahamas Speed Weeks proved his racing skills to the world. But neither his day job nor his weekend one seemed capable of taking him the next step. What he liked about both careers was that he traveled and met people.

One of those people, as Paul Van Valkenburgh chronicled in *Chevrolet = Racing . . .?*, was George McKean who, according to Van Valkenburgh, became a close personal friend. McKean owned a successful automobile dealership in Philadelphia, Pennsylvania, and when he began to contemplate retirement, he offered his business to Penske. Roger's bankers and his insurance broker gave him a choice: their assistance or his racing. After an exceptional season in 1964, he retired at the height of his success.

But for Penske, stepping away from driving did not mean moving away from racing. He already had managed car prep for his Texas racing friend Jim Hall. He ran Hall's successful effort at Sebring in 1965. It wasn't long before he had the systems down—both at his new Chevrolet dealership and with Hall's Chaparral team. It was time to get back into racing for himself. He was a Chevy dealer and he had raced Chevrolet-powered cars. He called Zora Duntov, who suggested

he contact Dick Guldstrand. "Goldie," as everyone called him, had just won his second Pacific Coast SCCA Championship, both times in Corvettes. Duntov offered to make the introduction. "Deek," he said into the phone, "Deek! You know Meester Roger Penske?"

"What? Who? Who's Roger Penske?

"Deek, I want you to drive for him. He will call you and I want you to bring all the parts you've been developing to his shop and move to Pennsylvania."

"Well, Zora, who is this guy? Does he know what he's doing?"

"Deek, Deek, don't worry about that. . . ."

Guldstrand flew back to Philadelphia. He met Penske at the dealership in Newtown Square. They made a plan that included Roger hiring Dick as his first professional driver. After returning to Los Angeles to ship his things, Guldstrand made another trip for Penske. This time he went to the St. Louis Corvette plant to pick up their 1966 coupe.

"Zora wanted to win the twenty-four hours of Daytona," Guldstrand explained in a 2009 interview. For 1966 Daytona had switched from a set-distance 2,000-kilometer event to a 24-hour race. "Zora had this special four-twenty-seven engine. We got the first one in late 1965. Everybody was wondering what they were going to call it. It was the engine that had been built as the prototype and now it was given to us to run at Daytona."

A new L72 427-cubic-inch displacement and 425 horsepower engine already was available for 1966

The car raced in its original red at Daytona in February, winning the GT-over-3-liters class as car No. 6. In preparation for its run at Sebring six weeks later, Penske's team painted it Sunoco blue and changed its number to 9. It again won its class, GT-over-5-liters.

The winter drive across the country was brutal but fun for Guldstrand. He wrapped himself in furniture moving blankets to stay warm but got into a lot of little races in the small towns along the way.

Soon after picking up the car at the St. Louis plant, Guldstrand had to fill up the 36-gallon fuel tank. In those days of full-service gas stations, the attendant was certain gallons of gas were flowing out through a hole somewhere because the total kept rising.

Corvettes. Duntov anticipated the physical similarity between it and his prototype engine and thought it could slip past inspection scrutiny without discovery.

Engineering had completed nearly three years of development work on the L88 427-cubic-inch engine, the "Mark IV big-block." Duntov wanted to get it into production cars but others in Chevrolet were nervous about the risk. The engine developed 530 horsepower and about 530 pound-feet of torque. It was a racing engine. Chevrolet opted to offer it to "special people" once they knew these buyers planed to race it. That meant people like Penske, Guldstrand, and others. Guldstrand described the transfer of the car:

So I flew back to St. Louis to pick it up. It was the dead of winter, mid-January, 1966, awfully cold, really terrible weather. Here was this thing. They couldn't even get it to start! [There was no choke on the enormous 850-cubic-foot-per-minute Holley carburetor.] We were putting out the fire belching up over the windshield out of that big carburetor. And once I got it running I was supposed to drive this thing to Pennsylvania. . . .

Well, I did want to shake it down anyway. But it wouldn't even start. We pushed it off the end of the line and out into the parking lot. I got it running and they wrapped me in furniture blankets—it had no

heater, no radio. This was a race car. And off I went down the road.

The car had a thirty-six gallon gas tank. At the first service station I stopped, the poor bastard trying to fill it up kept looking underneath [the car]. He just knew there was gasoline running all over his driveway.

It was quite a ride, though. I had a lot of fun going across the country. Had a lot of races in little towns. And when I got to Pennsylvania, Penske gave this classic line. He looked at me and he said, "Goldie, what do you need to win?"

Talk about taking the amateur out of the boy. All of the sudden he got . . . me . . . any . . . thing . . . I . . . wanted . . .! He was in his Learjet day and night getting me whatever I needed whether it was bearings or headers or whatever.

That was the massive Penske organization at the time; there were four of us. And two small dogs. Scottie, Murph the Surf, Bill Mayberry, and me. I was the truck driver and test driver and I pulled engines and dropped other ones in and I drove the race car.

Penske immediately shipped the freshly broken-in prototype L88 engine back out to California. It went to Guldstrand's home town, Culver City, to engine builders Travers and Coons, TRACO. They evaluated the new engine and reduced its compression to

Guldstrand picked up the car at the St. Louis Assembly Plant *in mid-January. He drove it, without a heater—it was a race car—back to Roger Penske's shops outside Philadelphia.*

something more suitable for a twenty-four-hour endurance engine than a twelve-second drag race. They replaced parts and modified others and shipped the engine back. A second L88 engine direct from Chevrolet went through TRACO and arrived at Daytona for Penske and Guldstrand the day before the race.

"We'd built the car in the dead of winter, there was snow everywhere," Guldstrand recalled.

Every time we pulled away from anywhere, we got stuck in snow. We finally got to Florida. It was a hell of a drive, one of the worst winter storms in years and we kept thinking, "Thank God, we're going to Florida and it's going to be wonderful."

And we got there and it was twenty-eight degrees. So the first thing that happened, we unloaded the trailer and we got disqualified.

You know that line, "You never cheat until you're caught?"

We'd cut out the fenders so those big Firestone tires would fit underneath the wheel wells. We'd done all kind of stuff to get it light. They just looked at us and shook their heads: "Whadaya think yer doin'?"

So we had to start putting stuff back on the car. The car looked bad because most of the time we were trying to put it back together. They'd figured out what we'd done.

Scrutinizers made the team pop-rivet light aluminum strips onto the cut-away fender to restore the factory line. Guldstrand had to remove the 7-inch-wide wheels they had fitted and remount the original 6s. Inspectors began to look closely at the car. "It was blindingly fast. We were running one eighty-five, one ninety down that back straightaway, almost staying with the prototypes. And this was a production Corvette! It was really . . . really . . . fast.

"But we had issues with it. We had to make a funny little spoiler up front to hold it down. Penske is a smooth-talking devil when he wants to be and somehow he got us through all that and we made it to the grid. We'd been quick; we set some kind of track record for GT cars that lasted a long time."

They started from the 21st position on the grid, fastest of the Grand Touring qualifiers by nearly 20 seconds a lap and just 13 seconds slower than the

In the middle of the night, *Dick Guldstrand's co-driver crashed the coupe into the rear of another car on the banking, knocking off most of the front bodywork of the Sting Ray. Quick-thinking Chevy engineer Gib Hufstader racer-taped two large flashlights onto the car's front fenders, and driver Guldstrand chased a fast Ferrari till dawn.* Photo Courtesy of Kevin Mackay Collection

pole-winning Ford GT40 MK II prototype. Guldstrand drove the first shift and switched off with Penske's friends George Wintersteen and Ben Moore. The car ran away from the competition.

"Then Wintersteen crashed the thing about one o'clock in the morning," according to Guldstrand. He ran into the rear end of a Morgan +4 coming onto the banking and lost much of the front end of the car. Guldstrand was trying to sleep but the crew woke him.

"So I jumped in the car," Guldstrand recalled, "and drove right off the track! It was pitch black. There were no lights. There was nothing in front of the car. So I brought it back in and said I can't. . . .

"Penske said, 'Hey, are you a candy ass or are you a race driver? Get back in this thing.'

"So I headed out again and I just couldn't see anything. And then they black-flagged [us] or not having 'forward facing white lights.'" Guldstrand began to laugh. "Well, they were right. There was nothing there."

Chevy engineer Gib Hufstader grabbed the large flashlights that Sunoco R&D engineer Bill Preston had in a tool box and Penske's crew racer-taped them to the front fenders. At last they had "forward facing white lights."

"I went right off the track again," Guldstrand said, still laughing. "I mean, I still couldn't see anything. But I finally figured if I picked up on the lights of one of the prototypes, one of the Ferraris, that I could stay with them.

"I set another track record at two o'clock in the morning on the back end of a Ferrari. I was concentrating on his taillights because if I'd lost that guy, I was dead meat."

The car lost long moments in the pits two separate times in the small hours of the night. The first time was to remove the damage, and the second was to affix the flashlights and replace the radiator. One of the crew inadvertently punctured the original radiator as he was prying away crash damage. Penske and his crew scoured the paddock and found a new big-block 1966 Sting Ray. The owner was sleeping in the car.

"The story is they had to hold the guy down," Guldstrand said, his laughter increasing. "And they threw the radiator over the fence. But I really think the guy heard [our situation] and volunteered it. He wanted to be part of our effort.

"So I followed the taillights and set the lap record and then daylight came and we won the race." Guldstrand, Wintersteen, and Moore crossed the finish line in 12th place overall, first in Grand Touring over 3 liters. Despite the accident and the time in the pits, they beat the second-place GT car by 48 laps, 183 miles.

In a far less dramatic fashion, Wintersteen and Moore won their class at Sebring a month later. The car had raced at Daytona in its factory original Rally Red. For Sebring, Penske's sponsor Sunoco painted the car its corporate blue-and-yellow color scheme. (Guldstrand had joined Dick Thompson and the Jim Hall–owned/Penske–maintained Grand Sport 005, which retired following an accident on lap 65.)

After Sebring, Penske sold the Sunoco-blue L88 to Joe Welch, who raced it through the rest of 1966 as part of the "Penske team." Welch ran at Sebring in 1967 with George Wintersteen, but they finished too far back to be classified. The car continued to compete until 1972, when the next owner converted it to street use. East Coast racing historian and restorer Kevin Mackay located the car in 1983, but missed it when another enthusiast and vintage racer, Gene Schiavone, purchased it. Schiavone restored the car to Sebring 1967 condition. In mid-2002 Mackay was able to acquire the car shown here, and he and his staff at Corvette Repair, Inc. spent nine months returning it to the way it raced at Sebring 1966.

12

1973

CORVETTE SUMMER

TRANSFORMING THE LEGEND

"I wish I could tell you it came from some fascination with the Corvette," Matthew Robbins explained. Robbins was the co-writer, with his longtime friend Hal Barwood, of a motion picture originally titled *Stingray*, but which MGM released as *Corvette Summer*. Robbins directed the film and Barwood produced it.

It was really born as a story about a young man coming of age, learning some bitter truths about authority and affection. Its origins were in American drama rather than in American sheet metal.

I knew guys in my high school who really couldn't take part in anything other than auto shop, metal shop, wood shop. They had no interest in anything else. I remember that pretty well, and I thought it was interesting to put the focus on a bright guy who had a gift in that particular arena. He didn't have a father but he found one in his auto shop class. And then disillusionment ensues.

We really quickly settled on the idea of a project revolving around the restoration of a Corvette. Or the re-imagining of a Corvette by this tough-talking precocious mechanic-designer kid played by Mark Hamill.

"We developed this great theme," co-writer and producer Hal Barwood recalled. "To track down a car. Find it, make it his own. It gets stolen. Cars get stolen all the time. So we thought it would be his growth challenge, to find his stolen car. It was a quixotic task.

"We knew it had to be an iconic car. The iconic car is the Corvette." That choice inspired the film's original title, *Stingray*. "It referred to the car and to the theft," he added.

MGM "green lighted" the project and from that moment on, challenges and difficulties arose. This was the first film that was all theirs—script, direction, and production—and on this project, life imitated art.

"Once we started making the movie," Robbins explained, "we had all kinds of problems. We didn't have very much money [$2 million]. Not very much time [40 days]. The weather wasn't cooperative. It was a baptism by fire for Hal as producer and me as a director to come to grips with everything."

The pair quickly secured Mark Hamill's services to play Kenny Dantley, the auto shop wizard. Hamill was fresh off the first *Star Wars* film and he was becoming a hot commodity. Robbins and Barwood auditioned some 80 actresses before selecting Annie Potts (who went on to co-star on the television series *Designing Women*) to play the role of Vanessa, a young woman who hoped to become a Las Vegas prostitute. But the film had a third star—the Corvette. That casting choice involved many more people.

Legendary motion picture production designer Michael Haller had apprenticed a young talent named Jim Schoppe, who was ready for his first picture. Haller raced motorcycle sidecars and collected and

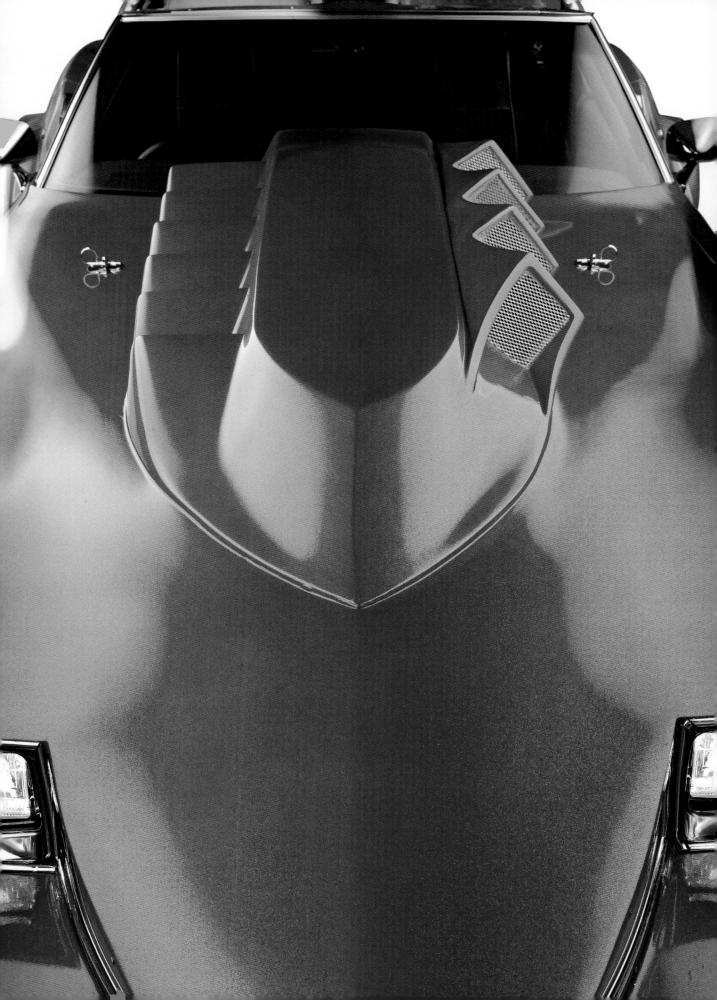

drove a variety of exotic and interesting automobiles, an interest he shared with Schoppe. When Schoppe landed the job as art director, Haller helped him conceive the car for the title role.

"Haller came up with the idea that we should make the car right-hand drive," Robbins said. "This was a huge issue. I thought, 'Do I dare?' But I thought it was so completely wacky and so arresting and so attention-getting that we would spend extra money and make it a right-hand drive Corvette! We did it partially for the impudence of putting the steering wheel on the right in the quintessential American car!"

Richard "Korky" Korkes, the car's builder, remembered there was another reason. Schoppe and Haller had explained it to him.

"They came up with the idea of right-hand drive," he recalled, "When Mark Hamill drove along Van Nuys Boulevard, if he was steering on the right hand side, he'd be closer to the curb to talk to the girls."

The film opens with Hamill and his auto shop class running around an auto salvage yard looking for a car they could repair. Hamill spots a 1973 Stingray in the claws of a crane swinging toward the jaws of a crusher. Sprinting to the crane operator's platform, he saves the badly wrecked car from its doom.

"The studio didn't want to own these cars," Korky continued. "They told me to buy two. They'd pay for the

conversion, so I gave them eighteen months exclusive rights to use them. After that, they reverted back to me. That's not typical in the business, but they were paying for the conversion to movie cars."

In one of the several instances of life imitating art, Korky purchased two wrecked cars for $3,000 each and set out to re-imagine them into what Schoppe had conceived in a couple of rough sketches he provided. Korky routinely worked with two automotive artists in southern California, Tom Daniels and Roy Jones, to better visualize his ideas. For this project, Jones developed a ¾ front and a ¾ rear view of the car. Korky took these to Schoppe, Robbins, and Barwood for their approval.

"Movie car assignments don't *come* to us," Korky explained. "We have to go to the studios and keep our ears open. I was dating an actress at the time. She came home one evening and told me there was a Corvette movie coming up. I went to John Dias, MGM's head of transportation. I already had done a couple projects for them and they knew me. For this picture, they wanted bids from four customizers."

Korky won the contract for $30,000 with the additional clause returning the cars to him 18 months later. He set to work building the two Corvettes for Hamill's character and two Firebirds for the villain. His crew finished one version of each, the "hero" or

"A" car, in great detail with attention to how paints reflected light as well as ensuring every feature of the car performed flawlessly. The "B" car, stunt car, or "second unit" cars were used for longer distance shots. Korky welded quarter-inch steel plate along the undercarriage of both "B" vehicles so they could jump or go over objects without damaging oil pans or gas tanks. "You always have to have a backup car," he said. "[If] something happens, you can't stop the movie."

One weekend, something did happen. In the film story, Hamill completed the car and everyone in his auto shop class got their turn to take it for a drive. One of the students returned from his drive on foot. The car had been stolen when he went into a store to buy soft drinks. This was the first crucial turning point in the film, the moment when Hamill/Kenny Dantley, the young man, set off on, as Robbins called it, "the quixotic task."

Robbins continued the story:

One morning in the last week of shooting, I came to the studio in Culver City. I'd been picked up early, before dawn, with director of photography Frank Stanley. We arrived at the lot and learned that there was this terrible excitement and panic in the motor pool. This was where all the studio picture vehicles were kept, cars for television shows as well as movies. All the vehicles for these productions were kept in the motor pool. The picture car, the 'A' car, our Corvette, had been stolen off the studio lot over the weekend.

I remember Frank Stanley, who was built like Santa Claus with a white beard and a big belly. He was sitting next to me in the back of the town car and he started shaking like a bowl of jelly. He was laughing.

At this point in the retelling, Robbins began to laugh.

My blood ran cold because I had so much work ahead to do. And this car was stolen. Not only was it stolen over the weekend, but it had been driven out the main gate of MGM. Which is to say that a guard who was on duty at two a.m. wrote down on his clipboard that the Stingray *picture car had been driven off the lot. He duly recorded this, and he remembered waving to whoever it* was behind the wheel!

Perhaps the car's most controversial design feature was making it right-hand-drive. "When Mark Hamill drove along Van Nuys Boulevard," Korky explained, "if he was steering on the right hand side, he'd be closer to the curb to talk to the girls."

Korky purchased two "wrecked" 1973 Corvettes from salvage yards for $3,000 each. He finished one carefully for close-ups and another served as a back-up car used for longer driving shots.

> *I did recognize how outrageous and ironic it was in a story about a stolen Corvette that the actual car had been stolen out of the studio. But I had all this work to do with the lead actors and now I had to shoot with the really not-picture-worthy second car.*

While Robbins frantically reorganized his plans for the day's filming in his mind, the cast and crew headed to the San Fernando Valley with the "B" car and they began to work. Around 2 p.m., he got a call. Police had found the "A" car parked about two miles from the studio on a side street in Culver City. A subterfuge not too different from the script's plot points emerged in the hours and days of investigations that followed.

"There had been a war—I was totally unaware of it— between some people in the transportation department of our picture and some of the stunt guys," Robbins went on. "They just didn't like each other. What seems to have happened was that someone on our picture was trying to get our head of transportation fired. So the idea was to

get that car unavailable for production for as many days as possible." Real life had inserted its own plot twist.

In many early scenes and in some later ones shot in Las Vegas, auto shops were primary shoot locations and centers of action. While Matthew Robbins had known guys in high school who lived in the shops, neither he nor Barwood were among them, and according to Korkes, there were inaccuracies in their script. In addition, Hamill had to appear competent working around the tools and the cars. Hamill became a frequent visitor to Korky's shop near Van Nuys airport as he learned the language and techniques of engine tuning and car bodywork. To be sure those scenes worked in the film, Barwood and Robbins hired Korky as technical adviser, recommending script terminology and actions for Hamill's character.

"Mark Hamill was a really bright guy," Korky recalled. "He caught on to everything quickly. He wanted things to look right. I remember in one scene he had to look like he was doing bodywork on the car; he

Korky faced a big challenge to turn a left-hand-drive Corvette into a right-hand-drive car. Initially he tried to reroute hydraulics but it became impossible, so he rigged a system using double-geared wheels and motorcycle chains.

In the script, the car was stolen from Hamill, a key element in his coming of age and dealing with disappointment and betrayal. Life imitated art early one morning when warring employees on the production stole the car from the MGM garages in the final week of shooting.

Then when he blew himself off, it looked real."

When he became the adviser on the film, Korky called all his suppliers. "I asked them how they would like to have Luke Skywalker from *Star Wars* use their product on screen." Truckloads arrived: wheels, tires, steering wheels, carburetors. "The engines were three-fifties but we hopped up the motors with all the parts my suppliers gave me, everything we could bolt on."

Michael Haller and Jim Schoppe had come up with the concept for the car that included its forward- and rear-facing air scoops. "We took a stock Corvette nose," Korky explained, "and built that scoop thing on top, filled in the seams, made cut outs to fit the Monza headlights. The back of the car was sheet metal epoxied into place. We did a big Chevy logo bowtie in the rear panel out of half-inch box tubing and Plexiglas lights. It lit up and said 'Stingray.' Then they learned they had to change the name."

The name of the film is something that still pains Robbins and Barwood decades later. A story in *Variety* magazine in late 1977 announced MGM's production of a film called *Stingray* for release in 1978.

"We screwed up, we didn't take care," Barwood recalled. "The name was in the piece. A sleazy

production company in the east or Midwest seized on it, figured they'd take advantage of the reams of publicity that MGM was bound to generate. When they decided to use the title, they had much shorter production time; the script was poor, the acting was poor. MGM's legal department stepped away. You can't copyright a title. You can register it, but MGM didn't want to pursue it."

"We were really young guys," Robbins continued. "We had no idea that such things could even happen. We had finished the picture. We were mixing the sound and one of the mixers was reading a trade paper. 'Oh guys,' he said, 'it's not called *Stingray* anymore.' We had our own Dantley moment."

The studio told them the title was to be *Corvette Summer*, because it was a summertime film for teenagers. MGM released it on June 2, 1978, using a "platform release plan."

"Great. What's that?" the two filmmakers asked during the marketing meeting.

"We're going to roll it out in a specialty marketing thing, start in the South, and build up from small towns and . . ."

This idea was Korky's.

Through his connections in the car world, Korky knew NASCAR founder Bill France. "My idea was to be

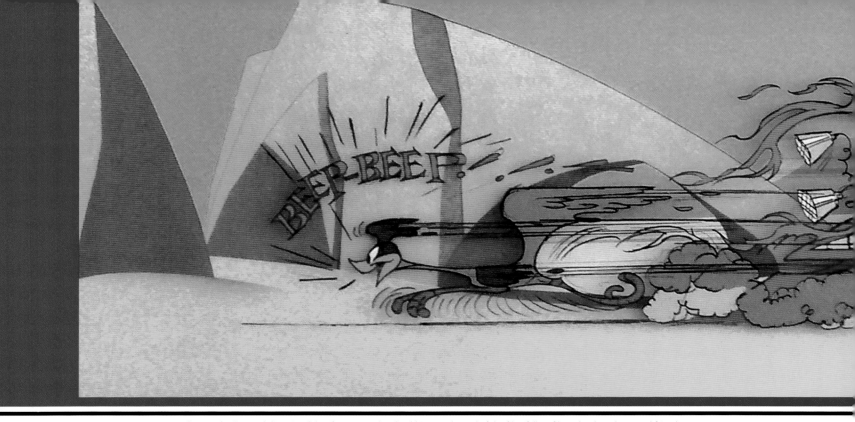

Corvette Summer *was the producing* and directing debut for Barwood and Robbins. At the end of the film, fellow film-school graduate and friend Steven Spielberg commissioned Hollywood animation artist Chuck Jones to create "a cheery 'Beep-Beep'" as a congratulatory gift. Hal Barwood collection

the first one to put together my type of promotion—for my work, my business—with a studio promotion. I called Bill France and asked him how he'd like to have the *Corvette Summer* car do a couple parade laps at each NASCAR race." France contacted a number of the tracks and got an enthusiastic response. MGM hired Korky for an additional fee to transport the car around the Southeast for several months. The "A" car ran a few laps and sat on static display throughout the weekend, surrounded by promotional materials showing Hamill and Potts on posters and in stills from the movie. Five days after each race, the picture opened in theaters surrounding the track.

The day filming wrapped, Hal Barwood had been watching the production for nearly six weeks. He then scratched an itch, hopped in the Corvette, and took it for a drive. In those days, a stretch of interstate north of Los Angeles, I-210, was finished but not opened to traffic. It became the filming location of choice for many television shows and movies.

"The car felt like a bucket of bolts," Barwood recalled, laughing. "It was a mess. I was pretty young and I drove it pretty fast. I was just praying the steering would hold

together. It was a movie car, not something you'd want to drive down the road. It's like everything in the movies. You just suspend reality and you don't realize how hard it was to see around those huge hood scoops."

Korky had tried to create a hydraulic steering system for the right-hand driving position but it was impossible with the budget and time available. (He'd had just 13 weeks to find and prepare the four cars.) "So we got rid of all the hydraulics," he recalled. "We left the steering box on the left side, and put gears on the shaft, mounted a steering wheel on the right side with a couple gears and looped two chains around it. We didn't want it to fail."

Korky got both cars back after the 18 months elapsed, and for several months he drove the "A" car. He remembered taking his actress girlfriend to the beach and to dinners in it. Sometime in 1980, he sold it to an enthusiast in Newport Beach. The "B" car went to Australia and then on to Japan, where laws permit only right-hand drive vehicles. A few years later, the "A" car joined a collection of Corvettes in Cooperstown, New York, at anthropologist Allen Schery's Corvette Americana Hall of Fame.

To MATTHEW AND Hah.
A CHEERY "BEEP-BEEP!" FROM CHUCK + STEVE
ON THE ADVENT OF FORMIDABLE DIRECTORIAL TEAM.
Chuck Jones
1977

In another of the ironies that infected the Robbins/Barwood script and film making, Robbins and his wife were delivering his daughter to college in upstate New York and passed a billboard announcing the museum and its opening day, August 25, 1992. He gaped at the sign, detoured to Cooperstown, and arrived in time for the celebration. Surrealistically, he introduced himself to Schery, who, having worked to prepare and promote the museum for several years, reacted as though he had expected Robbins' arrival all along and had no idea about the pure coincidence.

Robbins, who had wrestled hardest with the question of right-hand steering, never drove the car. During several chase scenes, he had ridden with the camera operator on the nose of a special vehicle, making sure they were getting what he wanted in the shot. "I sat on the prow of this rocketship right next to the camera and a young operator. We were chasing the car on a desert road. When we got the shot, we went back to the start mark. The operator was a tough, young, very savvy guy. He got out from behind the camera and looked at me. 'I'm sorry,' he said, 'I'm not doing this without hazard pay.' And he was serious." They had

reached speeds in excess of 100 miles per hour. "So, I never drove the car, but I do remember going very fast right behind it."

And what of the decision to make the car right-hand drive? Lines in the script that explained the modification got filmed but cut in editing.

"To this day," Robbins said, "I have never had anybody mention it or ask about it. I was so worried: What would all the Corvette owners have to say about this outrageous idea? It's like it never happened. You'd think that something like that, well, you can imagine sitting around and cooking it up! The enormity of the decision and the effort we put into it! And it was a complete non-issue."

When the Cooperstown museum shut down in June 1998, Mid-America Motorworks founder Mike Yager acquired the "A" car, the subject of this chapter. It's on display daily at MY Garage Museum in Effingham, Illinois. Korky produced a third copy of the car in 1992 for an enthusiast in Phoenix. He had to start from scratch; trash haulers in Van Nuys had erroneously picked up the molds for the original "A" and "B" car before filming had ended.

1976

JOHN GREENWOOD *SPIRIT OF LE MANS* CUSTOMER CAR #007

THE *BATMOBILE* IN FRANCE

The Auto Club de l'Ouest (ACO) runs the 24 Hours of Le Mans each year. This organization has enjoyed seeing U.S. entries and made an unusual effort in 1976 to encourage American entries. In the spirit of more than two centuries of brothers-in-arms camaraderie, the organizers decided to help celebrate the American Bicentennial in France.

Automotive journalist John Rettie reported on the race for *Road & Track* magazine in its October 1976 issue. He put the event in context. Le Mans had been the home of a 24-hour race since May 1923. However, interest among manufacturers, drivers, and spectators had ebbed. From the late 1960s into the early 1970s, the health of motorsports was in decline. ACO rule changes had blurred previous racing class distinctions. Early efforts at designing cars in wind tunnels had blurred distinctive shapes into similar aerodynamic streaks distinguishable only by color. The world's economy, exacerbated by Middle East petroleum politics, conspired to slow down the flow of entry forms and spectators to the race. The world needed a good party and the United States' birthday was a good cause.

"The Le Mans organizers," Rettie wrote, "have attempted to overcome the waning interest with some changes in the classes this year, with new categories for Group 6, 5, and 4 cars, unhomologated production cars (GTX) and Le Mans prototypes (GTP) built to special dimension and weight rules. Finally, through an agreement with Bill France and the Daytona

24-hour race, as well as in recognition of the American bicentennial, two NASCAR stockers and two IMSA GTs were invited to compete."

John Greenwood showed up with the No. 76 *Spirit of Le Mans* Corvette and Rettie reported that many observers said it was the best looking car in the race. The second IMSA car was Mike Keyser's Monza, fitted with a much larger rear wing for downforce along the long Mulsanne Straight. "Greenwood and Keyser have driven at Le Mans previously," Rettie continued, "so it was not an entirely new experience for them."

Competition, in fact, was old hat for John Greenwood by then. He had begun racing—on the streets of Detroit—around 1960, driving a 1955 Pontiac. A Chevy Impala with a 409 followed that and by 1964, he was in his first Corvette. In an interview in 1995 with historian Wayne Ellwood, Greenwood explained his racing roots:

"I just kept building them and racing them," he said. "I would tune my cars up every single night and go out and race about a hundred and fifty miles. I started putting bored-and-stroked four-oh-nines and NASCAR big blocks in my car. I kept building engines and changing them. I would sell the last one to build a new one. I was kind of driving my parents crazy. I built the engines in the basement or the den and then carried them up through the house."

When he was 18 or 20 (he couldn't recall exactly), he bought a silver 1964 Corvette. He dropped in an

The high camera angle accentuates the Coke-bottle silhouette of John Greenwood's wild bodywork. He introduced his "wide-body" racer at the Detroit International Automobile Show in December 1974.

John Greenwood was known for his attention to detail and the quality of his work. Everything was clean, tidy, and well organized in the cockpit and everywhere else.

early 427 after modifying the frame rail to fit it. Then he married and acquired a 435 horsepower 1968 coupe soon afterward.

"The first night I had it I put an L88 into it. My wife saw an ad for a parking lot autocross at the grocery store one day and dared me to enter. I did and won everything. I went back the next week and did the same. There were some pretty fancy cars because a whole bunch of road racers showed up with trailered cars, but I won again. So, I figured that since I could win, this wasn't a bad deal."

Greenwood grew up in the Detroit area. His father, a World War II fighter pilot, returned from the war and worked at GM's Tech Center. A local roadrace circuit, Waterford Hills, was familiar to engineers of all the automakers. The track offered a driver's school and the chief instructor named Frank Cipelli worked with Greenwood. By his own admission, Greenwood did not do well. "The guys instructing me did things differently that I was used to," he told Ellwood, "and I seemed to go backwards. There were women in Fiats beating me. I went through two sets of tires one weekend just trying to keep up."

He thought about the experience through the winter and formulated a plan. He was establishing his new race-engine business, Auto Research Engineering (ARE), but he also had a natural ability to tune suspensions and set up cars. He worked on his own car, returned to Waterford in 1969, and began setting records. He raced frequently in 1969, earning his regional and national racing licenses in the same year.

"In the next two years, I won the SCCA A-Production National Championships back-to-back," he continued. "You know that a lot of the equation was the big engines. I learned on Woodward Avenue that you don't want to get left behind on the straight parts." Through 1970 and 1971, Greenwood ran his 1969 coupe (converted to a roadster for the 1970 season). He acquired a second roadster in 1971 for long-distance events. Both cars were tremendously successful.

His connection to instructor Frank Cipelli led to a major sponsorship arrangement with tire manufacturer B.F. Goodrich (BFG), announced in the spring of 1971. Cipelli was the manager of Michigan International Speedway (MIS) at the time. He had done consulting work for BFG, knew the cars John and his brother Burt

Journalists at the debut in Detroit immediately nicknamed the car "The Batmobile." The front and rear wide fender flares were the work of GM stylist Randy Wittine, who used them as aerodynamic downforce aids.

were building, and made the introduction. Greenwood produced three cars for BFG that ran the long-distance races through 1972 and 1973 seasons on new-generation high-performance street-radials. When that contract ended in 1973, Greenwood switched to racing tires from Goodyear. He continued work on new concepts for cars.

"The wide-body or 'slab-side' cars were the next evolution after our Greenwood team cars," John told Wayne Ellwood. "The wide-body car was first introduced at the Detroit car show in Cobo Hall in 1974. It was dubbed the *Batmobile* by the press. . . . It was destined to be a 'team' car."

Greenwood developed the car's wheel flares with help from Zora Duntov, Jerry Palmer, and Randy Wittine. "Zora was always eager to help with ideas and to explore new concepts. Randy Wittine did the aerodynamics and styling stuff. Jerry Palmer, who eventually became head of Styling, also worked on them. Randy was involved in most anything that happened. . . . And of course, this was when we started dealing with Bob Riley for help with chassis design.

"The wide body had a very 'chiseled' front end. The IMSA rules didn't say anything about the fender flares,

so we shaped them to add downforce and left the back ends open." He and Burt fitted four-piston disc brake calipers all around and used a tube-type roll cage to help stiffen the chassis. The cars had a belly pan with a wing built just above the ground. "I guess it was an early form of diffuser," Greenwood explained, "and would have generated ground effects. IMSA rules didn't allow it, but that was okay because we knew it was going to be a sacrificial element in the rules game anyway. We did get away with the wheelwells being vented through the rear openings and that helped reduce lift."

By this time Zora Duntov was involved. He introduced Greenwood to a number of people in GM Styling. Randy Wittine designed extremely wide fenders that swept upward toward the rear of the car. These added downforce by using that extra surface required to cover wider wheels.

"We also added a lot of body rake to further add to the downforce. Our noses were so low because we dropped the body around the frame," recalled Greenwood.

Bob Riley did initial chassis work. Greenwood played with different settings over the next two years but eventually he returned to what Riley had set from the

Greenwood's **Spirit of Le Mans** *car (foreground) was a "customer car," which carried over a production based rear suspension. The more radical Spirit of Sebring (background) fitted a fully independent coil-over suspension at all four corners.*

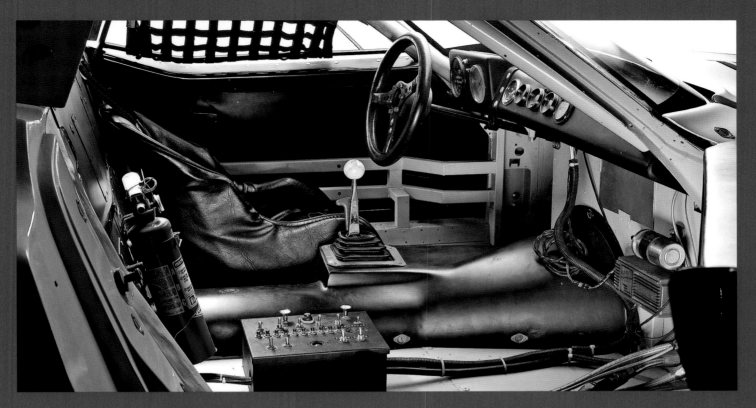

Greenwood's preparation was tidy and professional. *He worked with his brother Burt for decades producing highly competitive cars and winning races himself.*

For Le Mans, Greenwood fitted *his new cross-ram induction system to a car belonging to customer Rick Mancuso. The engine reportedly developed 1,000 horsepower, sufficient to push the car down the Mulsanne straight at 215.6 miles per hour.*

start. The car won the class championship and took the season finale with a two-lap margin over second place.

"After our wins in 1974, the Porsches and BMWs adopted our flared and open-wheelwell style but we still kept winning. We took class again in 1975. A lot of the older cars started to update to the wide body style and some bought our coil-over [shock absorber-style] rear suspension. Some series required that the original springs be used but they didn't prohibit additional springs, so we would use one leaf out of the original transverse layout and add the coil-over suspension to really do the work. It met the rules."

Greenwood considered the height of his development at that time occurred in his 1975 and 1976 *Spirit of Sebring* cars. These incorporated a coil-over suspension at each corner. He built these two cars plus a third one from spare parts. The car started from the pole in 1975 and from third position in 1976.

Soon after that race, Greenwood got a phone call that would take his creation overseas. One of the individuals who took care of Greenwood and his staff when the BFG cars competed at Le Mans in 1972 and 1973 had risen through the ranks at ACO to become head of the organization.

"It was in the middle of the fuel crisis and they were looking for a new draw to bring in the crowds. The American effort had been a big hit and our big-blocks had always driven the crowds wild. When I got the call, [Monsieur Froget] offered me lots of support to come over. It didn't matter if we ran well or even finished— they needed the draw! I figured out the cost and then doubled it. They paid because it was the two hundredth anniversary of the USA, and the stars and stripes paint scheme promised to be a big attraction." The *Spirit of Le Mans* image included a French soldier.

John and Burt had no suitable cars ready to race because the FIA didn't accept the coil-over suspension cars. However a "customer car," one built from scratch as a total Greenwood racer, was in the shop for updates. It had a "stock" rear suspension. It was Le Mans–legal. It belonged to suburban Chicago sports car dealer and racer Rick Mancuso, who agreed to loan it to John for the race. The Greenwoods installed their new cross ram induction system and a few other upgrades and they went to France. John Rettie's race report painted the scene:

Four o'clock Saturday came with the temperature in the nineties, the organizers counting the crowd to see if the new Le Mans had drawn the people in, the drivers complaining about the heat and Bill France with the start's flag in his hand. . . . John Greenwood was starting in ninth position after demonstrating in practice that his Corvette might not be the quickest through the corners but he could outrun everyone down the three-mile Mulsanne straight where he was clocked at 215.6 mph!"

The two IMSA entries, Greenwood's Corvette and [Mike] Keyser's Monza, were having a race of their won back about the 10th position and putting on a good show for the spectators. It was brief, however, as the Monza broke a halfshaft on lap 12 and Keyser spent the rest of the 24 hours selling Camel GT T-shirts. The *Spirit of LeMans* gave up the ghost 17 laps later, after just 144 miles. Tire problems had vexed the car during practice and qualifying and they proved to be its undoing. At speed a rear tire blew, demolishing some of the rear bodywork and taking some of the fuel cell with it. One account said that after his wild ride to bring what remained of the car to a halt, co-driver Bernard Darniche got out and hugged the ground.

One key figure in the drama was missing through the race weekend. Car owner Rick Mancuso had acquired the car at Sebring in 1976. In those days he was working for his father who, at the time, owned several dealerships throughout the Chicago area. When Greenwood asked him for permission to race the car— the subject of this chapter—at Le Mans, Mancuso went to his father to request time off to go watch his car in the race. The senior Mancuso said no.

Mancuso continued to race the car through the 1978 season in IMSA before selling it to Pennsylvania racer Kerry Hitt, who ran Trans-Am with the car for another few years. Hitt modified the car to suit his driving style. The car drifted into retirement and reached restorer Paul Canary in Santa Paula, California. With Hitt's help, Canary restored it to its original specifications. The car changed hands again before ending up in its present home with collector Steve Goldin in Florida in 1994, next to Greenwood's 1976 *Spirit of Sebring*.

Over his career, John Greenwood earned admiration and considerable support for Chevrolet. Engineers Zora Duntov and Gib Hufstader, and stylists Randy Wittine and eventual styling chief Jerry Palmer all provided assistance and advice.

GM stylist/designer Randy Wittine created the prominent front and rear wheel flares that contributed to the car's aerodynamics. John and Burt Greenwood lowered the body on the frame, dropping the "chiseled front end" to increase body rake which increased the downforce. Rules allowed them to leave fender flares open at the rear which reduced lift.

1978

COUPE INDIANAPOLIS PACE CAR

ESTABLISHING A NEW LEGEND IN 500 MILES

There was no doubt Corvette had become a General Motors success. Even for a niche product inside the corporation's largest division, its production numbers climbed steadily since 1970's 17,316 units. The renamed Stingray (now one word instead of two) had become less the severe sports car it was through 1967, evolving into a grand touring machine. Production in 1971 reached 21,801 cars, 27,004 for 1972, 30,464 for 1973, and jumped to 37,502 in 1974. Of these, Chevrolet fitted only 3,493 with the last big-block engine, the LS4 with 454 cubic inches of displacement and 270 horsepower. Production increased to 38,465 in 1975, which was the year Chevrolet stopped offering convertible Corvettes. Curiously, without an open car in the lineup, production increased in 1976 reaching 46,558 coupes and then 49,213 in 1977. Corvettes no longer had anything near the 430 horsepower of L88 427-cubic-inch engines. The most powerful offering for 1977 was the 210-horsepower 350-cubic-inch L82.

Corvette enthusiasts followed rumors of mid-engines and Wankel-engines in next-generation models. Zora Duntov made no secret of his desire for and belief in mid-engine placement, even after the early 1960s Q-transaxle concept faded into archival oblivion. Concept cars parading through major auto shows did much to keep interest alive and hope eternal.

An XP-880 grew and took form in Chevrolet's Engineering R&D department in 1968. Jim Musser took over command of R&D in 1966 when Frank

Winchell retired, and Musser carried on the idea of a mid-mounted V-8 set backward into the Y-shaped steel backbone frame. This positioned the engine's water pump near a large radiator mounted at the rear of the car. For the New York Auto Show in early 1968, the design staff named the car Astro II. It resembled Porsche's 904 and Bill Mitchell's Corvair-powered Monza GT, two influential designs from the early 1960s.

For the New York Auto Show in 1970, Chevrolet offered the XP-882, another mid-engine concept. Engineers mounted this V-8 engine transversely beneath a louvered, tapered boat-tail-like rear window similar to the 1963 Sting Ray.

Wankel engines, popular among engineers for their packaging capabilities, appeared in a twin-rotor 1973 Chevrolet GT. Its public debut took place not in New York but at the Frankfurt International Motor Show in September 1973. When OPEC (the Organization of Petroleum Exporting Countries) tightened oil supplies to the rest of the world, the marginal fuel economy of the Wankel short-circuited further development, but not before the 1970 XP-882 returned to Design for an update with a four-rotor version of the Wankel. Engineer Gib Hufstader packaged the rotary beneath sleek lines that designer Henry Haga had created, incorporating an articulating gull-wing door. It debuted at the Paris Salon de l'Automobile in October 1973, one month after the two-rotor car.

Chevrolet added more than $4,000 to the price of a base Sport Coupe to create the 1978 Indianapolis 500 Pace Car replica, taking the manufacturer's suggested retail price up to $13,653.21. It was the first Corvette to break the $10,000 price barrier.

Power for the actual pace car came from a barely-modified L82 350-cubic-inch 220-horsepower V-8. The car (and its identical back-up) ran headers and straight exhausts with reinforced automatic transmissions.

Communications with race control are crucial, but long gone were the days of massive radio receivers. Instead, the Speedway mounted a compact walkie-talkie under the passenger-side cargo cover wired to headsets for driver Jim Rathman and his co-pilot.

Bill Mitchell reclaimed the four-rotor XP-882 after the auto shows had finished and he had Design engineers install a regular production 400-cubic-inch Chevrolet V-8. The next round of auto shows proudly displayed the "Aerovette" and this time it seemed to be more real than previous flights of fantasy. Word seeped out of GM that soon after the board named him chairman on December 1, 1974, Thomas Murphy had approved the Aerovette, despite needing further development to make it easier and more economical to assemble, for production as the 1980 Corvette.

However, support steadily drifted away—into retirement, that is. Ed Cole retired at the end of September 1974. Zora Duntov went out three months later on New Year's Eve. Bill Mitchell left in July 1977. James Roche, a man with no engineering background and few ties to Chevrolet Division, succeeded Cole; Dave McLellan stepped into Duntov's shoes and his preference for front-engine Corvettes already was clear. GM, having had four decades of bombastic design leaders, pushed back against that trend and on August 1, 1977, the board named Irvin Rybicki as V.P. of Design. Rybicki was a man with neither the

vigorous personality nor the necessary friends that Earl and Mitchell had had. He was the answer to management's prayers.

The mid-engine car died. For Corvette enthusiasts, however, there was still reason for celebration. On March 15, 1977, not even five months before Mitchell retired, Chevrolet general manager Robert Lund celebrated the completion of the 500,000th Corvette, driving it off the St. Louis assembly line. What's more, throughout the aging plant, assembly line workers knew an updated and slightly redesigned car was coming for 1978, the 25th anniversary year.

"Corvette performance had taken a big hit," Dave McLellan wrote in his book, *Corvette from the Inside,* "but so had the performance of every other car sold in America." Between growing concerns over clean air and fuel economy, engineers had to strangle the engines and then bottle them up with a catalytic converter at the back end.

"On top of this," McLellan explained, "customers were consistently complaining about the fit and finish coming out of the St. Louis assembly plant. The C-3 was a tough body design to build, having been thrown

Initially, Chevrolet announced plans to assemble just 300 Pace Car replicas, which launched a collector frenzy and massive dealer price mark-ups. To appease customers and dealers alike, Chevy revised production up to 6,502, one car for each dealer.

together late and implemented with inadequate resources. The plant built the bodies, but in order to make things fit, they kept adjusting their fixtures until the body parts were as much as ¼ to ½ inch out of position. The plant would sometimes put repair on top of repair until frustration set in and the car was finally shipped."

According to McLellan, Chevrolet's division accountants were sure the sports car was losing money for Chevrolet. Few of General Motors' highest managers were engineers; they came from business and marketing backgrounds. The accountants had an easy time getting their voices heard. Their articulate presentations made it difficult for engineers and designers to do more than fixes and freshening on the 10-year old C3. Worse, their praise of profits forced the Division to increase prices on the cars in order to meet expectations within the corporation.

"So to get the Corvette future started again," McLellan continued, "we raised its price. Over the next nine years, accounting for inflation, we doubled the price of the car . . . we had little choice: The car's very future was at stake."

With few financial resources available, engineers and designers struggled to find a way to signify and celebrate the Corvette's 25th anniversary. The fastest, easiest, and least costly solution was to revise the roof by trimming back the "flying buttress" panels that surrounded the rear window. Early proposals for the C3 had included a functional fastback/hatchback rear window. Designers and engineers planned to resurrect the idea and introduce it on the 1978 model.

The new roofline brightened the cockpit and eliminated the claustrophobic sensation some owners had complained about with the earlier cars. It dramatically improved rear-quarter visibility. Access through a lift-up rear window was a stillborn idea, however, defeated by concerns the accountants raised over the costs of hinges and hardware. Automotive journalist Brock Yates found a different perspective:

"The entire fastback project opened Pandora's box for Corvette chief engineer Dave McLellan and his small staff," Yates wrote in the October 1977 issue of *Car and Driver*. "Obviously they were aware of the benefits of a full hatchback version, but given the restriction of the aged Corvette rear-suspension layout—the same hulking, rather undistinguished leaf-spring independent unit introduced in 1963—and its attendant high frame-rail kickup, their options were severely limited."

Allocating space for the fuel tank, suspension, a spare tire, and dual mufflers left little extra for cargo. "Money was not available for a complete redesign of the car aft of the seats," Yates continued, so McLellan and his staff enlarged storage space from 7.8 usable cubic feet in 1977 to 8.4 hidden under a retractable cover for 1978. They also expanded the 16.5 gallon gas tank to 24 gallons. It took some bending and flexing of rear frame rails, a slightly different spring assembly, and smaller mufflers to make it work.

Other improvements slipped past those who monitored expenses. The coefficient of drag (Cd) of the early C3s was 0.50 despite its sleek appearance. McLellan's engineers got a full-size model of the new car into the wind tunnel and found that a modest chin spoiler and an angled ducktail just aft the gas filler cap dropped the Cd to 0.42. These apparatuses also reduced the Corvette's notorious front lift and did a better job of holding down the rear end.

Before retiring, Bill Mitchell suggested to Jerry Palmer, the Design staff's Corvette designer, that Chevrolet should do a silver anniversary commemorative car in his favorite car color, silver. Palmer put his own flourish on the idea, painting the car silver over charcoal gray and adding a red stripe that rimmed the car's "belt line."

To honor the Corvette's 25th year, Chevrolet public relations approached Indianapolis Motor Speedway. They proposed the Speedway select the silver/gray 25th anniversary version as the official pace car for the 1978 race, Indy's 63rd running.

Carl Fisher, founder of Indianapolis Motor Speedway, had the idea that beginning a long distance race from a rolling start was safer and more exciting for spectators. He began, with the inaugural race in 1911, using an "official pace maker" to control the speeds of the 33 cars behind him. Fisher was the driver for the first five years, piloting an assortment of Stoddard-Daytons, a Stutz, and a Packard. By 1916 the honor had passed to significant automakers or experienced auto racers. Fisher interrupted the race for World Wars

To honor Corvette's 25th year, Chevrolet public relations proposed a commemorative edition as the Indianapolis 500 race official pace car. Originally, the car was to be the 25th Anniversary silver/grey combination, but Chevrolet asked Tony Hulman and other board members to devise a new color scheme.

Front row qualifiers lined up behind the pace car *for this publicity photograph. Pole sitter Tom Sneva (right), second fastest Danny Ongais (center), and third quickest Rick Mears (left) posed with Sneva's racer in the background.* Courtesy of Indianapolis Motor Speedway

I and II, skipping 1917 and 1918, and 1942 through 1945. Racer Wilbur Shaw drove the first Chevrolet, a 1948 Stylemaster Six. The second, a Bel Air, appeared in 1955. Another 12 years passed before Chevrolet's Camaro paced the event in 1967 and again in 1969. No Corvette had appeared there yet.

Ron McQueeney, a long time Corvette enthusiast, joined Indianapolis Motor Speedway in 1972 as a part-time photographer and in 1974 he moved to full-time work there. In 1977, the Speedway named him director of photography. He remembered discussions he heard—and overheard—in 1977 about the 25th anniversary car and the race. McQueeney remembered:

Originally, the 1978 Pace Car was to be the twenty-fifth Anniversary coupe, silver over charcoal. We heard it was going to be twelve to thirteen thousand dollars, including the decals. So I went out and ordered one. Right away. A couple weeks after that I heard rumblings about a special edition. And I figured I had already had a signed contract for it!

Then Chevrolet came back to Tony Hulman and a couple of his associates on the board. They asked Tony and the others to form a committee to decide a color scheme for the pace car. And they did. The committee decided the color scheme. And it wasn't silver over charcoal!

McQueeney went back to his dealer and tried to cancel his order. A contract was a contract, he was told.

Chevrolet's experience with pace cars at Indianapolis had not trained them well for what followed the official announcement. In 1955, Chevrolet general sales manager Tom Keating had driven the 180-horsepower 265-cubic-inch convertible around the speedway. No one went to a Chevy dealer asking to buy a replica of the car Keating had used. But by 1967, sales and marketing managers for Chevrolet and other companies had recognized and seized a trend: interest in a link to an event.

In 1958, Pontiac, running a 310-horsepower 370-cubic-inch V-8, produced an additional 200 "pace

The new rear roof line offered Corvette owners *many improvements including additional luggage space and nearly 50 percent more fuel capacity. It also dramatically improved rear visibility—important when 33 hungry Indy racers are following.*

car replicas" for racers in the NASCAR Convertibles series. By the time 1961 Indy winner Sam Hanks piloted the 1963 413-cubic-inch 360-horsepower Chrysler 300 convertible around the track, Chrysler had announced it would assemble 1,861 replicas. In 1967, three-time winner (and Corvette engineer) Mauri Rose drove Chevy's new Camaro with a prototype 396-cubic-inch 375-horsepower engine. Chevrolet had committed to manufacture just 100 replicas.

Two years later, Camaro again got pace car honors but this time, while the modified 396 still put out 375 horsepower, Chevrolet manufactured 3,675 clones. For several years after that, GM cars paced the race and each division determined its offshoots: Cadillac produced none; Buick manufactured as many as 1,290, and Oldsmobile offered 380. Chevrolet, hoping to keep the edition limited, wrestled among product planners and advertising account executives with numbers between 1,000 and 2,500. Chevrolet announced the base coupe at $9,351.89 and the pace car version was $13,653.21. The dealers loved it. Indy

photo director McQueeney remembered hearing from a salesman he knew that they were nearly doubling sticker price: $25,000.

"When it was announced," Dave McLellan explained, "late in the fall of 1977, a feeding frenzy ensued. Most pace car programs are lucky to sell two hundred replicas. Here we were, with people breaking past security to personally deliver checks . . . in hopes of getting on the list to buy one.

"In the end," he continued, "after consulting with the legal department, it was decided that a pace car should be offered to every American and Canadian Chevrolet dealer. That meant that Chevrolet had to build 6,502 cars." There went the exclusivity.

Pacing the start of the race has evolved over the years since the first one in 1911. From then through the early 1950s, racers followed a pace car on a single warm-up lap and then the race began. In 1957, the pace car led the racers on two warm-up laps. In 1974, that changed again with the pace car running two 75-mile-per-hour parade laps and a 90-mile-per-hour pace lap

The new roofline—specifically the larger back window—brightened the interior. This also eliminated a sense of claustrophobia some earlier buyers had felt inside earlier C3s.

just before the start. During yellow flag laps, the pace car held a 110-to-120-mile-per-hour rate, necessary to keep racers' tires gripping effectively.

An accident in 1971, when the pace car, driven by a local dealer, hit a photographer's stand at the end of pit lane, led the Speedway to allow only experienced racers into pace cars. For several years after that and including 1978, Indy 500 winner (in 1960) and Chevrolet dealer Jim Rathmann did the honors. As had been the practice for several years, the manufacturer whose car was selected for the race provided two identical vehicles in case of a mechanical problem at any time. Each of the cars used a minimally modified L82 engine and Chevrolet's three-speed Turbo Hydra-Matic automatic transmission. Indy management told Chevrolet that past pace car drivers had gotten so excited they forgot to shift. Indy insisted on automatics. Chevrolet punched two holes in the rear quarter panels so race officials could mount a yellow flag and a green flag. Under the rear locker cover behind the passenger, race management mounted a walkie-talkie wired to one headset for Rathmann and a second one for his co-driver. Chevrolet did so well with its preparation of the primary car that the backup never saw a moment on the track. Perhaps that was a hint at the fate of the replicas.

"When the flag dropped on May 26, 1978," McLellan wrote, "for the start of the Indianapolis 500-mile race, interest in the pace car fell off precipitously, and the speculators who had been instrumental in driving the market to dizzying heights, were now confronted with pace cars selling at a discount."

McQueeney had been frustrated, then disappointed, and finally he was relieved. Before race day, he took delivery of his silver/charcoal 25th Anniversary coupe—then a $399 paint option—at manufacturer's suggested retail.

Decades later, only one of the 1978 Indianapolis 500 Official Pace Cars has held its value. It is the car that is the subject of this chapter, the car Jim Rathmann drove as fast as 120 miles per hour on May 28, 1978. To this day, it remains at the Indianapolis Motor Speedway Hall of Fame Museum, a part of their extensive collection of their pace cars, race winners, and other special vehicles.

Indianapolis 500 Mile race winner—and five-time pace car driver—Jim Rathman steered the Corvette into Turn One on one of the pre-green-flag parade laps. Eventually, Rathman took the field traveling up to 125 miles per hour, before diving into the pits just before the start. Courtesy of Indianapolis Motor Speedway.

1981

COUPE #31611

ENDING AN ERA: THE LAST ST. LOUIS CORVETTE

It started with an off-hand, end of the day question from a couple of visitors to the plant manager. During the National Corvette Restorers Society (NCRS) convention in St. Louis, Missouri, in mid-June 1981, the organization had displayed four cars inside the St. Louis assembly plant. The oldest was a 1954, among the first cars assembled there, and the latest was a recently manufactured 1981 model year coupe. Plant superintendent Lou Ellebrecht had welcomed the cars and NCRS members during their visit. The organization had chosen St. Louis for its national meet to celebrate—and mourn—the end of production there.

Chevrolet became a part of General Motors in 1917. GM built a 1.6 million-square-foot plant in St. Louis and production started there in 1919. For a time, GM's board considered doing all its auto assembly out of that plant because of its location near the center of the country. The Mississippi River provided transportation for raw materials in and finished vehicles out, as did a number of railways. The term "transportation hub" could have defined St. Louis for many decades. The plant grew again and again but, by the mid-1970s, the facility was land-locked. Home-owners and businesses that surrounded it were unwilling to relocate so the plant could expand. More significantly, the St. Louis paint shops could not meet the Environmental Protection Agency (EPA) regulations that went into effect in the early 1980s. With no room to expand and a plant working nearly at capacity, GM either had to

close the paint shops for two years to renovate, or move. Relocation was the only practical solution. GM chairman Thomas Murphy announced the decision in March 1979.

A large operation in Bowling Green, Kentucky, that belonged to Chrysler Motors for producing air conditioning systems was available and GM acquired it in 1978 without letting on to customers or auto assemblers what its purpose was to be. It was the new home of the Corvette when it opened early in 1981. But in the interim, construction workers literally moved earth, floors, and walls to make it functional.

By 1980, St. Louis Assembly's days were numbered. David Burroughs, while researching factory practices for a 1965 396 convertible he was restoring, had visited the plant several times that year. That car ended up among the four on NCRS display. At the end of one of the tours plant employees gave to NCRS visitors in June, he and John Amgwert asked Lou Ellebrecht if he knew what the vehicle identification number might be of the final Corvette they would produce there. Ellebrecht paused, said he'd check, and he found the two men some time later, reciting the number 31616 to them. Burroughs, president of Bloomington Gold, watched as Amgwert, editor of *The Corvette Restorer*, the NCRS quarterly magazine, dutifully recorded the number in his notebook.

A week or so later, Ellebrecht phoned Burroughs to update information. The last car would be serial

Three historians who chronicled the St. Louis plant's assembly of its last Corvette learned the car was destined to go to a dealer who did not know its significance. The three quickly pooled their funds and bought the car to preserve it and keep it from becoming a "grocery getter."

Corvette assembly at the St. Louis plant took 22 hours, nearly three full work shifts per car. Body manufacture, from creating the passenger compartment birdcage through final paint finishing consumed two-thirds of the time.

number 611, not 616. Burroughs asked if anyone was documenting the assembly of the final car. Ellebrecht said he was sure Chevrolet would have photographers there when the car drove off the line. No, Burroughs meant through the entire assembly. Ellebrecht said he'd get back to him. A short time later, Burroughs had approval. During the NCRS June meeting, Lou had granted him and Amgwert the highly-treasured "photo pass," allowing them to take pictures anywhere without supervision. Now they had a mission. David called Amgwert and they added Corvette restorer Mike Hanson to their team. Hanson had been with Burroughs on a number of his 1965 restoration fact-finding trips.

Among restorers, there are thousands of questions. Most begin with: How did they do . . . whatever it was . . . at the factory? For Burroughs, Amgwert, and Hanson, this was the last chance to record precisely how that plant *did* do things, so all future St. Louis–car restorers would know.

Burroughs had another question for Ellebrecht: Where the car was going? The superintendent checked his records. Ed Rinke Chevrolet in Warren, Michigan, was the receiving dealer. That made sense. Rinke was Chevrolet's largest Corvette dealer at that time, his son Fred had a collection, and Burroughs and Amgwert assumed this last car was destined for that group of well-preserved cars.

Corvette assembly at the St. Louis plant required 22 hours, nearly three full work shifts per car. Burroughs arrived moments before 10 a.m. on Wednesday, July 29, 1981. He'd heard from Ellebrecht that 31611 would be in the "building buck" at 10. He raced through the plant and was relieved to find workers finishing up the second-to-last "birdcage."

The central core of the Corvette is called the birdcage because the network of frame rails that make up the passenger cockpit resembles a human-scale cage. Assemblers placed pieces of steel into fixtures

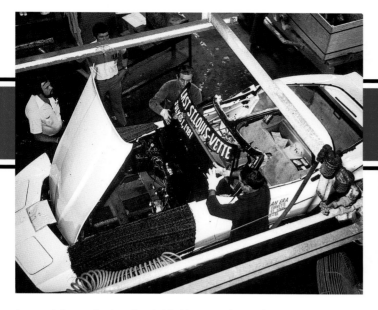

It was a delicate task to install a windshield in a C3. This crew had painted the windshield but knowing how often one cracks during mounting, they prepared a second one as well. © John Amgwert collection 1981/2009

The 190-horsepower L81 V-8 was the only engine available for 1981 from either the St. Louis or Bowling Green plants. Historian David Burroughs made a template of the windshield text for later recreation, knowing it would be scrubbed clean during the "water test" after final assembly.

and welded them by hand. It was quick work and within ten minutes, the welders were done with 31611. Burroughs notes read "10:07 cage assembly." Another 20 minutes saw the birdcage dunked into cleaning baths and sprayed with primer. The crew left it on the floor, drying and curing in the air while they resumed work on birdcages completed earlier in the day.

It was after 1 p.m. when they returned to 31611. Burroughs recorded, "2:03 cage transferred to assembly line," where the floor was welded in. Work at two additional stations ended the day at 2:30 p.m. That evening, Hanson and Amgwert arrived and the three planned their coverage. Amgwert and Hanson photographed everything from opposite sides while Burroughs took notes and recorded times, procedures, and the names of every single worker who touched the car.

Thursday started early: "6:16 front end body installed; 6:32 rear end body installed; 7:40 doors installed. . . ." They encountered a worker named Ray Barnes who had been at St. Louis since the 1950s. He had installed trim tags on tens of thousands of Corvettes. For 31611, he had a special one, "Last Corvette Built in St. Louis, MO. 7-31-81." According to

Burroughs notes, as Barnes secretly mounted it under the front passenger-side fender well at 1:44 p.m. He had told no one of the tag except the three visitors.

It was a day of exceptional behavior, a mix of Irish wake and celebration, of poignant memories and new moments. As assembly line employees learned what the three men were doing, they told stories and pointed out others who had special jobs the men needed to know about. There were signs everywhere saying "Going Out in Style." The plant was closing but no one had relaxed their attention to detail, or their concern for quality. Bowling Green already had opened and manufactured its first Corvette on June 1. However, it was a matter of Missouri pride that their final cars would be better than anything that ever would come from Kentucky.

By Friday morning, according to Burroughs and Amgwert, the factory held a sense of the last day of high school. Impala and Caprice manufacture had ended there a couple of years before and only Chevrolet pick-up trucks remained on the line. Still, workers from every part of the plant appeared, jostled and joked with their friends, and picked up an air wrench or screw gun to add their own effort to this final automobile. Ellebrecht, reflecting the corporate line, had forbidden

Chevrolet got a lot of life out of the C3 body, introducing it in 1968 and carrying it through the 1982 model year. Those were challenging years for the auto industry with oil embargoes raising gasoline prices, and the introduction of exhaust emissions and crash-safety standards.

The final production run of 1981 St. Louis cars all came with Camel interiors as the plant used up the last of its supply. The initial buyers and the current owners have kept the car as delivered from the transporter, with seat, steering wheel, and floor protection still in place.

With news media and plant management looking on, Marvin Lloyd defied rules and rushed up to label and sign the car before he lowered the finished body onto the engine and chassis in a process called the marriage. Historian John Amgwert's initials are visible near Lloyd's left hand. © John Amgwert collection 1981/2010

employees from writing on or signing the car. Dozens did it anyway, surreptitiously slipping up to scrawl their names on panels soon covered by liners, cowls, or insulation.

At 11 a.m. Friday, the engine and chassis came on the line. Body assembly, with its complex of fiberglass panels requiring intricate finishing even before the task of installing the serpentine wiring harness, took nearly two days. In body assembly, one of the installers had neatly painted "Last St. Louis Vette," and the date in white on a windshield. Being an experienced installer, he repeated the legend on a second one. Windshields were a high-risk installation and workers, no matter how careful, sometimes shattered their initial attempt. No one was taking chances with this car. Soon after, assemblers taped a pair of heavy cardboard signs to the doors: *End of an Era*, they read.

The chassis and engine were almost a blink in time in comparison to body assembly. From the first cars at Flint and continuing through St. Louis, the chassis went together upside down on a travelling form. "10:26 frame transferred to chassis building buck (upside down); 10:29 front and rear suspension installed; 10:45 chassis installation—exhaust pipes, brakes, fuel/brake lines, etc." Suspension and running gear were more easily attached by pushing down rather than straining up. Within an hour, the chassis was prepared for its

next major phases and mechanical arms flipped it like a child's toy. It was ready for its marriage with the engine, and later, with the body.

Ellebrecht and other managers waited for the media to arrive. Local newspapers, national wire services, and CBS Network News were there to cover the birth of the final car. "12:10 CBS television begins filming; 12:17 engine drop for installation into chassis." Burroughs notes missed no increments in the process. Marvin Lloyd, the man who controlled the winches that lowered the body onto the chassis, waited until everyone was ready. Then, with Ellebrecht watching and cameras rolling and clicking, Lloyd dashed up to the car body and scrawled "Last St. Louis Corvette" in yellow crayon on the underside of the luggage compartment. Everyone laughed and then came the applause. "1:06 body drop to chassis; 1:10 wheels installed." Lloyd did his job perfectly and the car settled at a theatrically slow pace without incident. Bolts got tightened and two of the plant's most senior employees who were retiring that day, Whitey Juergensmeyer and Cleo Hagar, got into the car, fired it up, and drove it off the line.

Out of camera range, they parked the car and shut it off. Officially, they completed the final car on Friday, July 31, 1980. However it still needed final trim and processing; this was work that waited until Saturday

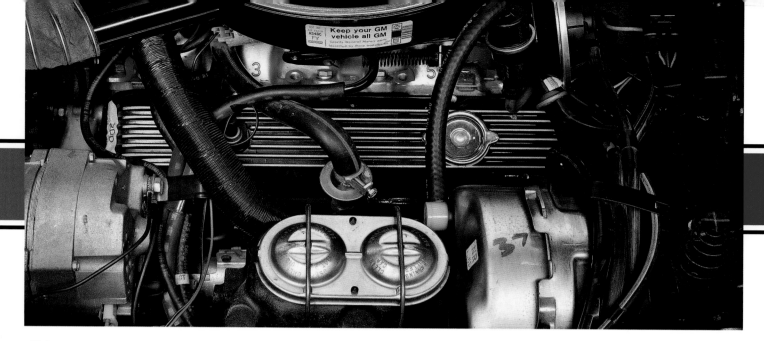

This is a restorer's dream come true. *Restorers always wonder how the factory "did it." This car is a time capsule, unmolested and unmodified and under nearly constant scrutiny since St. Louis finished it on July 31, 1981.*

morning. Hundreds of lights began to shut down. The plant that had been noisy and active since late 1953 fell quiet.

Cars had moved through the Corvette assembly on a moving tram towed by a chain. After this last car, the tram had another assignment: All the tools and eventually the tooling went to Bowling Green. Two trolleys behind 31611 carried large plywood boxes to transfer the tooling and equipment from the line. Shift supervisors followed the car with clipboards. At its peak in 1979, the plant operated with 1,450 employees manufacturing Corvettes. The population was less than half that by July 1981; in March, Chevy discontinued a second assembly shift as it prepared for shutdown. As each employee finished his or her work, they disconnected their tools from air or electric power lines, showed the serial numbers to their supervisor, and set the tools into the big box. Forklifts maneuvered the huge crates into two railroad box cars rolled into the plant. Another large sign followed. Someone had written the production total and a challenge: "695,138 Corvettes! Top That, Bowling Green!" Just before he slid the boxcar door closed, Ellebrecht set the sign upright inside the rail car.

The large plant became a ghost town as workers said their goodbyes and filed out into the afternoon sunlight. Everyone on the large workforce had been offered a transfer to the new plant in Kentucky. Nearly 1,500 of them accepted, uprooting their lives, families, and homes with a moving allowance from Chevrolet ranging from $500 to $1,200.

The supervisors had been too efficient. Typically, after "final" assembly, the cars got their interiors installed followed by a "roll" test and a "water" test, essentially a high-pressure wash to check for leaks. In any auto assembly process, some things malfunction and when the crew finished with the interior Saturday morning, the repair team discovered several small problems needing repairs. But their tools were in the box cars! They found what they needed, fixed a coolant leak, and then repaired a paint crack in the driver's side quarter panel. The car went onto the chassis dynamometer and ran up to 60 miles per hour for a few moments, then drove into the water test booth where the painted legend on the windshield sheeted away under the force of the spray. Amgwert and Burroughs each got short rides over the one-mile drive from the plant to the storage yard, where transporters loaded up the cars for delivery.

"It's like a funeral here," Gordon Drees, the inspection general foreman, told Burroughs. It was hot, bright, dry, and calm, not a breath of wind on a brilliant blue day, weather that made it difficult to reconcile everyone's mood outside with life inside the dreary old plant.

Assembly ended at St. Louis on July 31, 1981, two months after production had begun at Corvette's new plant at Bowling Green. "It's like a funeral here," the inspection general foreman Gordon Drees told a visitor.

As Amgwert, Hanson, and Burroughs packed up their cameras and notepads, they agreed their job was nearly done. They decided to telephone Rinke Chevrolet to ask if someone would photograph them unloading and delivering the last St. Louis Corvette. Amgwert volunteered to make the call.

"I called Fred Rinke," John recalled recently. "I asked him if he could photograph the last car as it came off the transporter. 'What last car?' he asked, 'What are you talking about?'

"I thought really quickly, and asked him if he had a car coming in that was number 31611?"

"He got back on the phone a minute later and said, 'Yeah, a beige coupe. Beige cloth interior. For stock. You wanna buy it?'"

Amgwert maintained his cool and told Rinke he'd take it! Then he hurriedly phoned Burroughs. Together

with friends Don Ellefsen and Fred Frederick, the four men scrambled together the financing.

"We were afraid someone else would buy it, not knowing what it was, and use it to get groceries and go to work and. . . . We had to preserve it!"

"Don't clean it up," Amgwert told Rinke when he called back to seal the deal.

Three weeks after it left the assembly line, Amgwert and Burroughs saw 31611 again in Michigan. Burroughs ducked his head under the fender and spied Ray Barnes' plate. By 9:30 a.m. August 22, they owned the car. It had 4.4 miles on the odometer when they loaded it on their trailer and headed off to central Illinois. It had every piece of plastic and paper protection still in place, just as it left St. Louis.

Over the next several years, Burroughs displayed the car at Bloomington Gold. His detailed notes had

The last Corvette assembled at St. Louis moved through the plant followed by two large boxes. Here a worker prepares to bond the nose of the car to the birdcage. Behind him, those who have completed their work set their tools into shipping boxes bound for the new plant at Bowling Green, Kentucky. © John Amgwert collection 1981/2010

included a template of the windshield legend and the cardboard door signs which he re-created soon after it went into his garage.

By 1986, the St. Louis car had graduated to Bloomington's Special Collection tent. That year, Burroughs had invited William and Kevin Adams, a father and son Corvette collecting team, to display a car for the first time. They specialized in ultra-low mileage factory originals, preserved the way Burroughs and Amgwert had saved the St. Louis car. They returned in 1987 and 1988, each time with new "sealed-in-plastic" cars—commemoratives, pace cars, collector editions— protected in the same way they left the factory. William and Kevin had seen the St. Louis car, and William confided to his son that if it ever came available, it would be an important addition to their collection. He approached Burroughs, but Burroughs politely declined.

Two months later, however, Burroughs contacted William. Acknowledging the quality and emphasis of their collection, he offered them the car. He and his partners had other needs for the investment capital the car represented. Within days, the deal was done. Over the next decade, the Adams' returned the car to Bloomington and its status graduated from the Special Collection into the organization's Hall of Fame in 1997. Around 31611, their collection grew as they continued adding brandnew factory-delivered Corvettes. They located and acquired the first car manufactured at Bowling Green, produced two months before the car that is the subject of this chapter was assembled. After one final appearance in Bloomington's Special Collection in 1999, William and Kevin Adams put the last St. Louis car away, preserving history once again.

1988

CALLAWAY SLEDGEHAMMER

TESTING OUR OWN CALCULATIONS

"When you look back at all the great automobiles of the past," Reeves Callaway said, "there is one thread that runs through them all. It's amazingly simple: They were one individual's vision of what the automobile should be, whether it was Duesenberg or Ferrari, Cord or Kurtis. And the closer they got to that vision, the better the car was."

Callaway's earliest recollection of his engineering interest and his mechanical bent was removing the engine from the family lawnmower and mounting it on a tricycle. He put engines on bicycles, then built go-karts and raced them "and then, ASAP, got into cars."

His ambition was to be world driving champion. After college at Amherst (which had no engineering program; he graduated with a fine arts degree), he swerved back to his ambition and went to work as factory text driver and race driver for Autodynamics, a race car builder in Massachusetts. There he took the first step in his driving career: Callaway won the Formula Vee national championship and waited for Roger Penske to call with a job offer. In quick succession, Autodynamics went broke, he nearly followed, and "magically," he recalled, "Bob Bondurant called and said he wanted to start a school and he needed instructors who could drive and teach." Callaway was uncertain of his teaching skills but he accepted the offer. BMW had hired Bondurant to instruct dealers how to drive their new 320i coupe and his itinerant band of racers taught novices at every racetrack in the country.

When the program ended, Callaway had become friends with everyone in the BMW program and he asked "if I could buy one of the tired, used-up street cars. I think it could use another one hundred horsepower," he explained. He took it to his home in Connecticut (which had no garage) and figured out how to strap a very rudimentary turbocharger system onto the car. (Autodynamics had assembled a couple of turbocharged cars for Pikes Peak while he was there.)

The finished car looked better than "strapped-on," and he loaned it to Don Sherman who was writing for *Car and Driver*. Sherman produced a one-page story that ran in late 1977, which made Callaway sound as if he were ready to ship kits out the door. "I didn't even have a drill press," he recalled in an interview in 2009.

He gathered some neighborhood friends and for the next five years turned out reliable, powerful kits that also met emissions standards. Callaway built a reputation that caught Don Black's attention. Black was the manager of Alfa Romeo U.S.A, which was watching Maserati's Bi-Turbo run away from them in performance and sales.

"Don asked if we could turbocharge the GTV-Six, do it emissions-compliant, do it to Alfa Original Equipment standards. Well, we think so [I answered]. But do you think it will hold together?"

That was the good news, Black told Callaway. The engine, to everyone's surprise, was really strong. He challenged Callaway to run a 200-hour full-throttle

Chevrolet's more than 20-year relationship with Reeves Callaway began with a phone call to Callaway from Corvette chief engineer Dave McLellan. Chevy had changed directions on a turbocharging project for production Corvettes but didn't want to lose the technology even it if meant creating a competitor.

At 253 miles per hour, the Callaway Sledgehammer was a blur across the Ohio countryside. The speed has not been equaled. Photograph © D. Randy Riggs 1988/2010

engine test. They did and went ahead with the project, beginning production immediately.

"The car was blisteringly fast and fun. We got one to Dennis Siminitis at *Road & Track*. We got thirty or thirty-five out the door and Alfa pulled the car out of the North American market." Callaway's first "OE" relationship evaporated. He had moved manufacture from his home into an industrial complex. It was late 1985 and he wondered what was next.

The answer had been percolating a thousand miles away for nearly several years. Since 1981, as Chevrolet and Corvette engineers prepared the C4 model, they had tested turbocharged V-8 engines. Engineers toyed with a V-6 for the Corvette to meet fuel-economy requirements. A Troy, Michigan, firm, Specialized Vehicles Inc., developed a prototype but Dave McLellan and others concluded that the V-6, which had vibration problems, was not the right image for Corvette. SVI began work on a V-8. By January 1985, they had a twin-turbocharged engine that developed 400 horsepower and 500 foot-pounds of torque.

This package had two problems: GM had no transmission that could handle that torque, and no one inside the corporation or within its customer base viewed turbocharging as a high-tech engine technology. To that point, turbos only had appeared on small imported engines and as aftermarket modifications on cars like the BMW and Alfa Romeo. General Motors had offered a turbo on its Corvair Monza "Corsa" in 1965 and 1966 and an Oldsmobile model had used a turbocharger in 1963. Even after tests showed the dramatic performance potential of such a Corvette V-8, Lloyd Reuss, Chevrolet's general manager, sent the team back to the drawing boards, muttering terms like "natural aspiration," "dual-overhead camshafts," and "four-valves per head." Within days, Don Runkle, Chevrolet's head of market planning, met with Dave McLellan, Corvette's chief engineer. It was May 1985, and Runkle had an idea.

"Lo and behold," Callaway said, "the phone rang and it was Dave McLellan at Chevrolet. 'We have an Alfa in our war room,' he said.

"'You have a Callaway Alfa?'

"'Yes, and this little two-and-a-half-liter turbo car is faster than our 1985 Corvette!'

"'Yeah! We know!' [I said.] And that was how it started with the Corvette! McLellan called us. It's always better if they call you."

McLellan and a group of engineers came to visit Callaway's operation in August and were impressed. They shipped one of their 16 prototype fuel-injected twin-turbos to Old Lyme. Chevrolet told Callaway they wanted 400 horsepower, 0-to-60 in five seconds, and a top speed of at least 170 miles per hour. Callaway and his engineers looked over the prototype, saved some stock pieces, pulled others from Chevrolet racing catalogs, and devised some brilliant solutions to the problems of moving air, locating turbos, and fitting twin intercoolers.

Writing about the collaboration with Callaway in his book *Corvette from the Inside*, McLellan explained why they reached out to a potential competitor.

"We pushed and shoved to get Corvette performance into the hands of our customers anywhere and anyway we could. If the four-cam normally aspirated project was killed along the way we would still have something to show for our earlier efforts. On the other hand, if the four-cam project succeeded, we would have spawned a competitor. And competitors only make you stronger!"

Callaway recalled his meeting with Runkle's marketing staff:

"GM asked how many we thought we should build.

"'How many do you think we can sell?'

"'What's the price?' they asked.

"To do what they wanted done," Callaway explained, "the car cost twenty-five thousand dollars in those days. And the engine cost another twenty-five thousand to turbocharge correctly. So here we had a fifty-thousand dollar Corvette. And that made their hair stand on end.

"'How could anyone . . .?' 'Who would pay . . .?' 'We can't . . .!'"

Callaway asked them how many they thought they could sell at $50,000. The answer came back before the question was out of his mouth: 25. So they tooled up for a production of 25 cars. In June 1986, Chevrolet assigned Callaway a regular production number, B2K, for their twin-turbo Corvette.

"And that's when the phones lit up. And they never went out for five years. We tooled up for twenty-five cars; we played catch-up for five years. We manufactured more than five hundred based on a twenty-five car plan." In 1987, Callaway produced 188 of their cars. Another 125 came out in 1988, 67 in 1989, 58 in 1990, and 71 in 1991 for a total of 597 cars over five years.

"It taught us a lot," Callaway said. "We thought in the beginning that we were doing an engineering job with and for GM. We were really getting a lesson in how to have a car company. We were not only manufacturing parts and producing cars but we were administering dealer relations, warranties, press representation, emissions compliance, foreign sales, and international government regulations. . . ."

Dave McLellan wanted to have the Corvette become a platform that was respected by the rest of the automotive world. They had the talent and they had the money. They just didn't have the respect yet that he wanted.

Callaway knew that one technique to enhance a reputation was to get a car to Europe and to get it into the best car magazines there. He carefully established his European distribution not with any of GM's international dealers but with the best specialist maintenance shop there, Woehr & Ciccone. They prepped the car for European use and they got one to Germany's *Auto Motor und Sport* magazine, generally regarded as Europe's best. The red 1987 Twin-Turbo ended up on the cover.

A short time earlier, Mercedes-Benz's tuner AMG introduced a sedan they called the *Hammer*. *Auto Motor und Sport* disagreed. No, no, "*Das is der Hammer*," the cover headline read. McLellan and Callaway were ecstatic. Soon after that, the two men were on the phone, and Callaway commented on the cost of preparing a car for that kind of test.

"It cost about a million dollars to build a car for a magazine test. If you're really going to do it right, test it ourselves, get the tire companies on board. . . .

"I said, 'Why don't we just build one magazine car and just roll it out where there's a test? But we'll have to have an adjustable top speed so that it will run just fast enough to win the event and then we'll bring it back home.'

"'We bring these cars back,'" McLellan told him, "'and we crush them. They're built on prototype chassis, X-chassis.'

If top speed was all they were after, *Callaway believed a top-speed run car could be "civilized." This meant an air conditioned interior with a working radio, electric window lifts, electrically adjustable seats, and a roll bar of course.*

Chief engineer Tim Good called the car a rolling laboratory. "It has to be able to be driven to the store by your mom as well as go two-hundred-fifty miles an hour."

Tim Good told the test track engineer *"You don't understand. This car's supposed to go two hundred fifty miles an hour." The engineer snickered until two days later when the car clocked 254.76.*

"'Don't do that anymore.'" Callaway called a good customer and bought back his car. He turned it into a special project car. "Smartest thing I ever did. The definition of the project between McLellan and ourselves was, build a car that will always win, no matter who shows up, no matter who."

Cars in those days were struggling at the one-ninety- to two-hundred-mile-per-hour point. So we picked a target that was way beyond what we thought anybody ever would achieve. Why don't we go two-fifty?

Dave and I talked about it and he suggested that if the red car was "the Hammer," then this one was to be the Sledgehammer.

I asked him if he knew German slang? "Hammer" in German is not the same thing in English. On the street corner in Germany, a "hammer" is an erection. We had the "woodie," and we were about to have "the big woodie!"

Callaway's experiences driving another of his magazine-test winning cars, *The Top Gun*, redefined what these cars had to be. *Top Gun* was a thinly-disguised race car that was loud, unmanageable at low speeds, with noisy straight-cut gears and plastic windows. It was created for a *Car and Driver* comparison test in 1987 titled "A Gathering of Eagles." It had reached 231.1 miles per hour.

If top speed was all they were after, Callaway still believed their car could be civilized, with an air-conditioned interior, radio, glass roll-up windows, and a roll bar, of course. Over the next 12 months they figured

out how to make a car with an aircraft-like top speed. As chief engineer Tim Good said in an interview in 1988, "This was a rolling laboratory. It's not just a statement about top speed. It has to be able to be driven to the store by your mom as well as go two-hundred fifty miles an hour." When they finished their work, they climbed into the *Sledgehammer* on October 19, 1988. They drove it from the Old Lyme "home base" to the Transportation Research Center in East Liberty, Ohio, and their 7.5-mile high-speed test track. They had been there several times before during B2K development and for the Gathering of Eagles. Part of their travels this time, and the first day on the track, October 21, took place in rain. Contaminated fuel caused an intermittent engine misfire that for a while they misdiagnosed as an ignition problem.

"High speed testing is not really the fun you'd imagine it to be," Good continued.

We were testing the car and really starting to have trouble at the two-hundred and ten or fifteen mile per hour mark. The folks at the test track said "Well, gee, you know, the car seems to be working fine. What do you expect it to do, get a few more miles an hour?"

I turned to the test engineer who was sitting next to me who worked at the track and said, "No, no, you don't understand. This car's supposed to go two hundred fifty miles an hour."

He turned the other way and started snickering. And the whole attitude of people at the test track changed. They were not coming by the car anymore; there was no interest in the project any more. It was like having a disease.

Drag racer/Corvette builder John Lingenfelter stepped in for Reeves Callaway to do the final drive. When he finished, he smiled at Callaway's engineers and said, "You know, your car goes one hundred miles an hour faster than mine!"

The track management shifted Callaway's location to a corner of the shop. People who had been delegated to help became unavailable. Few people in Ohio believed the car was capable of going any faster.

The first run of the next day, October 26, was just above 248 miles per hour at nearly full throttle. At that point the test engineer looked at Good.

"Is that it? Or does this go any faster?"

"Oh, it'll go faster. . . ."

"Okay. We'll keep the track open."

The car pitted. It had been a cool afternoon with high clouds that closed in. "Tires look good, Reeves," a few people commented. Special tires, four only, rated to 300 miles per hour, had come from Goodyear. No one discussed the price. "Feels good," he replied. "Hands off. This car knows the way around." It was 3:45 p.m., getting dark in Eastern Standard Time. Track engineers wanted to shut down and go home. Callaway had relinquished the driving responsibility that day to

a friend with more experience, John Lingenfelter, who climbed back in the car and went out. A few minutes later the silver car shot past leaving in its wake a mix of engine noise and tire whoosh.

"It was then that we knew," Good said. The car reached 254.76 miles an hour. "And after that, they asked me if we wanted the track for more time to go any faster. No, we were pretty satisfied.

"John Lingenfelter was all smiles," Good said. "There were lots of congratulations and then John got into his standard Corvette and started to drive away. He stopped and rolled down his window. 'You know,' he said, 'your car goes one hundred miles an hour faster than mine.'"

"We weren't thinking about setting a record in that car," Reeves Callaway concluded. "We were testing our own calculations. We didn't do too well. We had figured the car would go two-fifty-two. It went two-fifty-four and three quarters. We screwed up somewhere."

2001

C5-R-003 LE MANS CLASS WINNER

BEATING THE WORLD'S BEST ON THEIR OWN TURF

C. Five. R.

Not RPO something.

Not Zee Oh Six.

Not a package of options, but a full-on, uncompromised, fifth-generation Corvette factory race car.

"The C5-R will be remembered like no other Corvette in history," Doug Duchart said in 2004. Chevrolet's director of racing continued: "We've not only improved the breed for the production car, but the racing program has proved tremendously valuable for what it has done to energize the corporation from the inside. From the moment of the car's first test at Grattan Raceway in 1997, it was destined to do great things."

GM engineers began the process of developing the C5-R to race in the FIA's GTS class more than a year before the car's introduction as a 1997 model.

"We selected the GTS category," Corvette chief engineer Dave Hill explained, "because the cars are more like road cars, the race courses are more like real roads, and manufacturers from all over the world compete there." Chevrolet's goal was to use the racing program to show off the handling and performance capabilities of the car both as a race car and a sports car. Chevrolet's motivation was to reclaim the title of "America's Sports Car" from the Dodge Viper which, while launched in 1992, began a successful racing career in 1996 with its GTS-R.

There were some critics who charged that the C3 and C4 generations had become more sporty luxury cars than sports cars. They accused Corvette product planners, designers, and engineers of losing their way as they tried to intercept and fight off sales challenges. European and Japanese manufacturers saw a market opportunity and focused sharply on what a car in this class should be. When GM committed to building a new Corvette—and gave Chevrolet the chance to start with the proverbial clean sheet of paper—it was a chance for the car to reclaim its place. Throughout its history, racing had improved the breed. But racing efforts sometimes came as afterthoughts and it often fell on outside engineers and competitors to find and capitalize on the car's potential. Here was an opportunity to promote the car and improve the breed from its point of inception.

Chevrolet chose to marry its in-house technology and efforts with outside operations, with whom they started work 18 months prior to the car's debut at the Specialty Equipment Manufacturer's Association (SEMA) trade show in November 1998. GM Motorsports manager Herb Fischel directed the project and one of his first appointees was Ken Brown, who had designed the C5 chassis and suspension systems for the production vehicle. Doug Fehan, named C5-R program manager, brought in Detroit-based Pratt & Miller and Riley & Scott from Indianapolis to develop and campaign the cars. (Bob Riley and Mark Scott performed chassis development work on the project through 1999 but then moved into Cadillac's Northstar

It's an aerodynamic masterpiece, with twin NACA ducts ingesting air while countless louvers expel warm air and highly pressurized air. Racing teams in the 1990s and 2000s were very much concerned with airflow management.

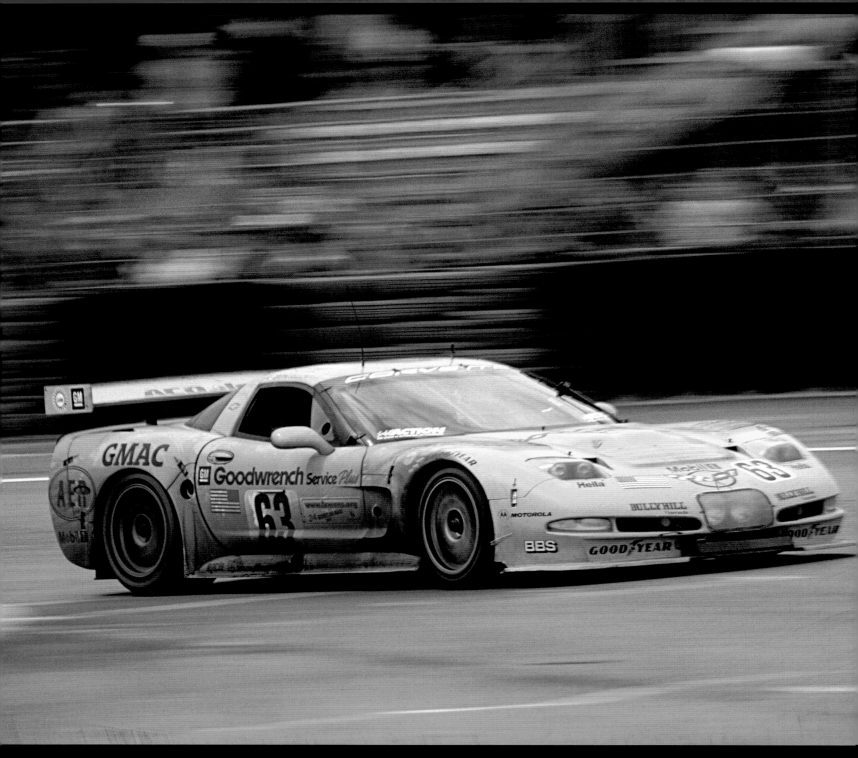

At the end of a long 24 hours, *Ron Fellows had shared the drive with Scott Pruett and Johnny O'Connell. Together they brought the Corvette across the Le Mans finish line. It*

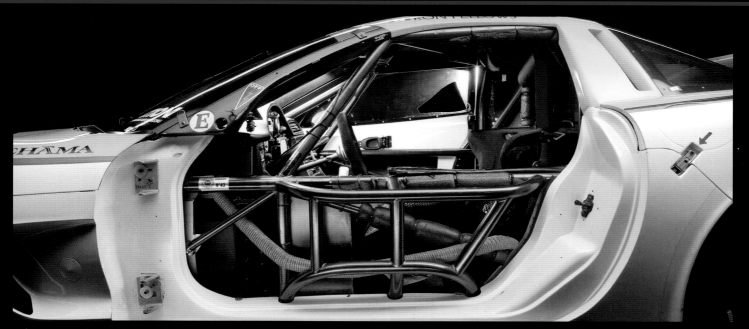

Driver entry and egress is somewhat obstructed: *Gymnasts only need apply. The tubing is not only for crash safety but also for making the car extremely stiff to improve handling.*

LMP—Le Mans Prototype—program in 2000. Riley & Scott were purchased by Reynard Motorsports which went bankrupt in 2001.)

"We're racing Corvettes because we have to," Fehan said, "it's the next logical step in the evolution. How else do you prove performance?" For Corvette, it meant going head-to-head against Dodge and, later, Ford in the Saleen cars. Necessity also bred a better race car. Chrysler Corporation had achieved what Chevrolet had turned its back on: international racing victories that included class victories at Le Mans starting in 1999. These siphoned attention and sales from the Corvette.

Gary Pratt and Jim Miller started with a completely stock C5 with steel hydro-formed chassis rails. They tore it down to its most fundamental components and reassembled it as the C5-R, a purpose-built machine that took great advantage of many regular-production components. Front and rear chassis cradles retained factory specifications. Stock hydro-formed frame side rails formed the base for the roll cage. The upper and lower front control arms, rear control arms, the steering rack, and power steering pump all were production pieces. The race car used the production windshield, taillights, and marker lights. The production engine

casting line produced unique castings for the race car, and the alternator and water pump were stock items.

"We tried to use as many common processes as we could in developing the race car," GM racing chassis specialist Ken Brown recalled. His engineers made extensive use of "our design tools, like finite element analysis and other computer-aided design/computer-aided manufacture (CAD/CAM). We even tried to use as many production suppliers as possible in our program."

Racing engineers very slightly changed the stock Corvette body to incorporate a few more aerodynamic advantages. The drag coefficient of the production car was 0.29, a low number for a road car, but better still, design work in wind tunnels prior to the car's release eliminated much of the aerodynamic lift that had plagued Corvettes generations earlier. This provided an excellent start point for aerodynamicist Brian Miller to design the wings and other devices that created additional downforce on the racer. "The racing Corvette," he explained, "produces so much downforce at speed that it could theoretically drive upside down on the ceiling of a tunnel."

Pratt & Miller stretched the C5 wheelbase by about ¼ inch, from 104.5 inches to 104.7. The body grew

Rear downforce came *not only from above but below. Undercar airflow has always been tricky; if mishandled it may cause the car to flip, but if done right as these rear diffusers reveal, the car hugs the road like a vacuum.*

179.7 inches to 182.8. They dropped the vehicle height 2 full inches, from 47.8 stock height to 45.8 inches and widened it nearly 3 inches, from 73.6 inches to 76.4.

P&M engineers started with a 6-liter 366-cubic-inch V-8 engine block with 4.125-inch bore and 3.42-inch stroke and worked it to develop about 600 horsepower at 7,200 rpm (in contrast to the LS1 346-cubic-inch production engine that put out 345 horsepower at the time.)

Through 1998, Ron Fellows, then the car's development driver, had put more than 4,000 miles on the "mule." "Handling is really key in endurance races," he explained in an interview in November 1998, "especially in the twenty-four hour races where conditions can change. We've done a lot of testing at Daytona and Sebring. For now, Corvette is content with competing in the U.S. [in 1999] on its quest to improve the breed. But international sports-car racing has been put on alert—beware the red bowtie at Le Mans."

Through the season, the team ran six of nine events in silver-and-black GM Goodwrench livery. By the end of the 1999 season, both C5-R-001 and C5-R-002 were running with even more potent 7-liter 427 aluminum-cast engines developing 590 horsepower, developed by Katech Performance in suburban Detroit.

For the 2000 racing season, Pratt & Miller introduced two new cars in the new yellow color scheme. Chassis C5-R-003 and 004 represented the evolution in their development. The team was ready to join the American Le Mans Series (ALMS) midway through and they struggled against competitors like Dodge Vipers and Ford-powered Saleens. All that changed at Texas Motor Speedway, where chassis 003 won its class, the first victory for the racing Corvettes. Both 003 and 004 continued to compete through the season.

The team owners planned a more ambitious—and full ALMS—schedule for 2001 and it started off tremendously. At Daytona, chassis 003 (car No. 3) won outright. This was a particularly sweet victory for Corvette because a Viper had been first overall the year before, just beating C5-R-003. For 2001, the nearest Viper finished in 31st place, nearly 450 miles behind the winners. Corvette No. 4, chassis 004, with Daytona regulars and NASCAR favorites Dale Earnhardt Sr. and Dale Jr. sharing driving duties with Andy Pilgrim and Kelly Collins came in fourth overall and second in GTS, 14 laps behind their teammates. Newspapers and magazines ignored Pilgrim and Collins and referred to the race and the victory as "the 24 Hours of Earnhardt." It was a race that was also nearly 24 hours in rain, an

To win GTS class, the Corvette completed 278 laps and covered 3,794.7 kilometers or 2,371.69 miles in 24 hours. The team of three drivers crossed the line in eight place overall.

unfamiliar condition for father and son. After the race, the older Earnhardt, who was accustomed to traffic on his way to seven NASCAR titles, compared driving the 24 Hours of Daytona to "New York, New York." Again in Texas, 003 took class honors, notching its second and third victories.

For Le Mans, engineers changed to a new flat rear wing that created less drag on the ultra-high-speed circuit. (Circuit engineers revised the long Mulsanne Straight as well, reducing the height of a hill that in 1999 had sent a Mercedes-Benz racer flipping upside down at speed. Even ground-effects became lift tendencies if adhesion to the ground failed.) Ron Fellows, Scott Pruett, and Johnny O'Connell, wearing the No. 63 reserved for European contests, completed 278 laps, to finish eighth overall, and first in GTS class. Pratt & Miller racked up Corvette's first class win at Le Mans since 1960 (in the Briggs Cunningham car that is the subject of Chapter Five in this book). Chassis 004, car No. 64, with Andy Pilgrim, Franck Freon, and Kelly Collins took second in class, finishing seven laps behind their teammates.

"I just hope that somewhere up there Zora Duntov is enjoying what is no doubt the greatest victory in Corvette history," Herb Fischel said.

"We really had to work for this one," Doug Fehan added. "Nothing comes easy to any race team. This has to be the toughest race in the world."

By this time, C5-R-003 had become Pratt & Miller's venerable workhorse. It won class again at Sears Point, in Sonoma, California; Portland, Oregon; Mosport, Ontario, Canada; and Mid-Ohio. Another round of rebuilds, updates, modifications, and improvements followed over the winter between the season-ender at Atlanta (in which C5-R-004 won,) and the 2002 ALMS season that commenced for the team at Sebring.

Before the summer had ended, Chevrolet, Pratt & Miller (for their chassis), and Katech (engines) announced plans to sell as many as five C5-R customer cars "to buyers with a passion for performance." By mid-August, they had accepted deposits from two individuals. Racers purchased the engine and electronics from Katech, which shipped those pieces to Pratt & Miller for installation.

At Sebring on March 16, 2002, Pratt & Miller again claimed the podium, coming across the line first in GTS, recording the ninth victory on this chassis. The team shipped 003 and 004 to Le Mans for the May 5 trials and stored them near the circuit until the race on

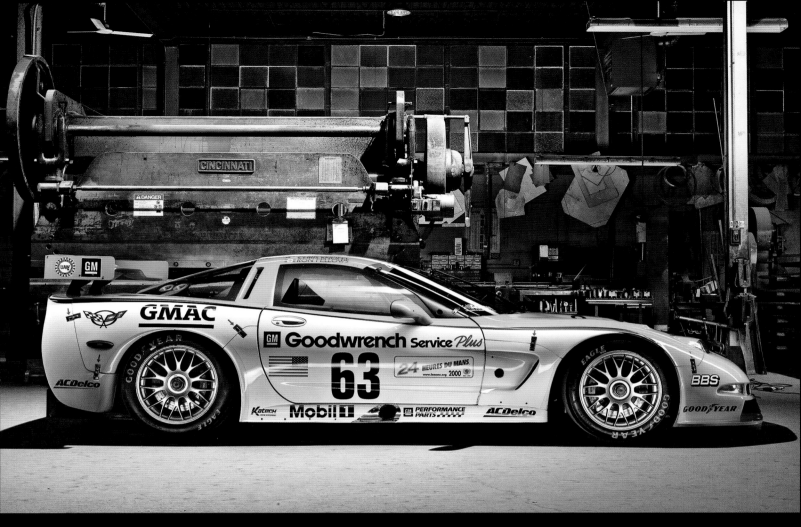

Pratt & Miller started with a completely stock C5 and tore it down to its most fundamental components, keeping what was useful and modifying or replacing other pieces. Portions of the instrument panel made the cut, and the C5R uses the production windshield as well.

June 15 and 16, when 003 again claimed class honors, the second straight Le Mans class win for 003 (and tenth victory for the car) and second place for 004 for Pratt & Miller.

The team continued the season with new cars, 005 and 006, introduced at Sears Point between the Le Mans trials and the 24-hour race there. While 003 and 004 made their way home, Pratt & Miller campaigned 005 and 006 though Mid-Ohio, Road America, Washington D.C., Quebec, Mosport, and Laguna Seca. The team had left 003 and 004 in their shops to be ready for Miami on October 5. This proved a wise strategy when a fire at Laguna badly damaged 005 and the team needed the extra week to prepare 005 and 006 for the season finale at Atlanta on October 12, 2002. Between the four cars—C5-R-003 (the subject of this chapter), 004, 005 and 006—Pratt & Miller, and drivers Ron Fellows, Johnny O'Connell, Franck Freon, and Oliver Gavin, 005 racked up five season victories and 006 took home two others. At the end of the 2002 season, Pratt & Miller sold C5-R-003 to a private collector in the Midwest.

The Katech Corvette engine develops more than 590 horsepower and is set well back in the chassis to improve handling. Cooling air, forced in below the two center driving lamps, exits through louvers and vents in the hood (about where the Corvette Racing logo appears) to assist the chin spoiler with front downforce.

2009

ZR1 #5900001 "BLUE DEVIL"

WITH JAKE, THE LEGEND IS IN GOOD HANDS

When the sixth-generation Corvette appeared in January 2004, it did not represent the startling change owners, enthusiasts, and journalists hoped to see. Chevrolet claimed that 85 percent of the car was new with parts not interchangeable with the C5. But after huge evolutions like C3 to C4, and then to C5, buyers had gotten spoiled. But it was nearly invisible chassis improvements and subtly enjoyable cockpit changes that counted as the big changes in the C6.

From the start, Corvette planners developed a succession of increasingly potent variations upward from the base coupe and convertible. Everything began with the 6-liter 400-horsepower LS1 V-8. The optional Z51 package turned a highly capable road car into a track-days dream with suspension upgrades; larger brake rotors; extra coolers for engine oil, transmission lube, and power steering fluid; quicker transmission ratios; and Goodyear asymmetrical EMT tires. Adding the Magnetic Selective Ride Control (MSRC) gave the car an uncanny ability to levitate over potholes yet respond instantly to other real-world and racetrack demands. The 2006 Z06 introduced the 505-horsepower LS7 427-cubic-inch V-8 and a host of suspension, body, and interior improvements. Base model, Z51, and Z06 improvements continued through 2007 and into 2008. At the same time, word spread that Chevrolet was bringing back the ZR1 designation introduced in the 1970s with the LT1. Corvette resurrected it for five glorious years in the

1990s with the monstrous Lotus-designed/Mercury Marine–assembled LT5.

Corvette writer and historian Richard Prince said it best in his overview of the first year C6 back in November 2004: "Power is at the top of every fan's wish list. . . ." The ZR1 took this Corvette off the wish list and made it a fantasy destination with its hyper-developed 6.2-liter, 376-cubic-inch supercharged LS9 that developed 638 horsepower.

Corvette engineers worked hard to give the Roots-type supercharger smooth response across the engine's full range. Typically these "bolt-on" boosters have less effect at higher engine speeds, and graphs of horsepower curves look more like ground-to-ground missiles than atmosphere-escaping rockets—but not this one. Peak horsepower in the LS9 occurred at engine red line, 6,500 rpm. From 3,000 rpm on, the harmony of engine combustion, supercharger whine, and exhaust roar was music to everyone's ears.

As writer Mike Monticello explained it in *Road & Track*'s road test of the car in its February 2009 issue, "With the supercharger's help down low, the ZR1 produced a never-ending forward surge of other-worldly power, the kind of rush that makes you laugh hysterically with every full-throttle run through the gears. The force of its acceleration," he continued, "actually makes you forget to breathe, and the violence with which it gobbles up blacktop – as though it hasn't eaten in months—startles passengers." The magazine

This is the third ZR1 designation in Corvette's lifetime. The first came in 1970 and stayed through 1972. The second reached buyers in 1990 and lasted through 1995. This third generation is the most radical, the most potent.

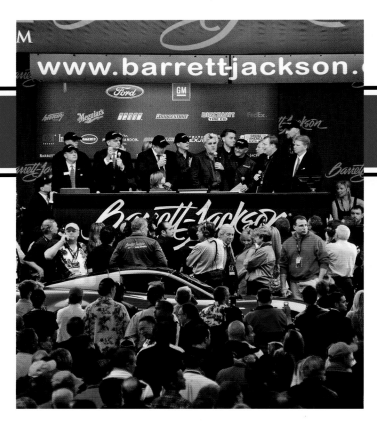

Historian Richard Prince said it best: "Power is at the top of every fan's wish list." With the ZR1, Chevrolet engineers gave them 638 horsepower out of the supercharged LS9.

Called "A Corvette on Steroids," *Barrett-Jackson auctioned lot number 1316 surrounded by a crowd that sensed something exciting was about to happen. Master of Ceremonies Jay Leno worked the audience, and by the time the gavel fell after two-and-a-half minutes of bidding, Chevrolet's first "retailable" ZR1 had sold for $1 million.*

posted 0-to-60-mile-per-hour times of 3.3 seconds while 0-to-120 miles per hour took 9.9. The standing start ¼-mile took 11.4 seconds at 125.5 miles per hour. Top speed was reported at 205 miles per hour. It was the most powerful and fastest automobile General Motors had ever manufactured and offered to the public.

Racer Sam Posey once likened the acceleration of another Corvette he was driving to the sensation a driver gets "as if the road suddenly plunged downhill." With the new ZR1, that sensation was more like nose-diving off the edge of a high cliff.

Through leaked photographs and press releases that hinted at the car's potential and its limited availability, Chevrolet masterfully built a fever among the "gotta have it" drivers and the "must own it" collectors. To take best advantage of that pulse-raising potential, Chevrolet turned the sale of the very first copy into a fundraising event.

"Want to be the first to get your hands on a new 2009 Corvette ZR1?" Ray Wert wrote on the online site Jalopnik on December 28, 2007. "Head on over to the Barrett-Jackson auction as we've just heard the first ZR1 will be going up for auction as part of their 'Muscle Car Wars' marketing.

"Lot Number 1316 – From rumor to instant legend in the blink of an eye, Chevrolet presents the very 'First Retailable Unit Built' for auction at Barrett-Jackson on Saturday, January 19, 2008 with all proceeds [beyond vehicle price] from the auction [going to] benefit The United Way."

Chevrolet produced a special vehicle identification number (VIN) sequence just for this car—5900001, one of the few times an automaker had created a new number range for a single vehicle, adding to the uniqueness of the car. The car carried a "Monroney," or price sticker that listed a $99,000 suggested retail price. The Monroney designated a limited production option (LPO) BD1, standing for "Blue Devil One." Designers and engineers inside Corvette nicknamed the car "Jake." It was painted Le Mans Blue Metallic, code 19U, the only example in that color in the 2009 model year.

In a classic understatement, Corvette's exterior design manager Kirk Bennion described the car his

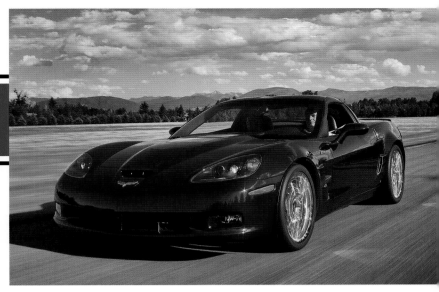

Writer **Sam Posey likened** Corvette acceleration to how a driver feels "as if the road suddenly plunged down hill." The ZR1 cockpit embraced and secured its drivers, coddling them in premium audio, air conditioning, and leather comfort.

Road & Track *magazine writer* Mike Monticello described the ZR1 performance: "The force of its acceleration actually makes you forget to breathe, and the violence with which it gobbles up blacktop—as though it hasn't eaten in months—startles passengers."

team had created. "There is nothing subtle about the ZR1. It's a car that isn't shy about its capabilities. . . . There is an aesthetic element to all the unique features, but they were developed first and foremost to support the car's performance capabilities."

Before the auction began in Scottsdale, Arizona, that night, auctioneer Craig Jackson and evening Master of Ceremonies Jay Leno worked the crowd into frenzy.

"For those of you who know Corvettes," Leno yelled into the microphone above the din, "you know this is the one Zora Arkus-Duntov would have built if he still were alive. This will go down in history as the greatest Corvette *in* history. You see that paint? Sixty thousand dollars a gallon! As many of you know, I'm president of the 'More Money than Brains' club and pretty much anything I want I can get. I wanted the best Corvette and I bought a Z06 and then they came out with this. And now I gotta get one of these too! But the nicest thing is, I could have four or five of these for the price of some of my other cars and, pardon my language, this will kick their ass!"

Leno referred to the value of owning car number 001 of any make and mused into the microphone about the value of 1953 number 001. Jackson looked across the audience and spotted a friend and former bidder,

Dave Ressler, who had purchased 1953 number 003—the oldest known Corvette—from him two years earlier. Jackson then asked Ressler where *he'd* like to start the bidding.

From Ressler's shout of $100,000, it took eight seconds for the price to reach half a million. Everyone in the large audience sensed something big was happening. The atmosphere was a blend of carnival and cocktail party. Bidding stalled for 25 seconds at $600,000, then jumped to $800,000 in another two seconds. Two bidders had kept the action alive, moving it—in 70 seconds—from zero to $900,000, where it suddenly appeared stalled. Leno cajoled two front row bidders who had been sitting on their hands.

Standing beside Leno, Troy Clark, GM North America president, confirmed the details: Le Mans Blue, VIN number 001, a unique Regular Production Option (RPO) BD1 that was retired after the car was assembled, factory delivery at Bowling Green. Jay chimed in, offering to let the winner pick up the car at his garage in California so he might get a chance to drive it!

Spanky Assiter, Jackson's livestock-sale fast-talking auctioneer began calling for one million dollars, trying to get the program moving again. The spotter in front

of Ressler slipped on a Ressler CollectorCorvettes.com jacket and watched his bidder. Ressler pulled a dark blue ZR1 logo ball cap onto his head. Then he waved his arm in a wide sweeping overhead gesture.

"One million dollars!" Jackson called out. The bidder who had taken it to $900,000 had just raised his own bid.

Ressler had been a Chevrolet dealer since 1977, starting at the same dealership where his father Chris had worked for 25 years in Mandan, North Dakota. Shortly after Chris died, Dave joined the staff. The owner offered to sell him the dealership in 1988 and Dave stepped up, turning the agency around and repaying his backers in 18 months. It became North Dakota's biggest and best Chevrolet dealership. His hard work—by the time of the auction he also owned dealerships in Montana—had put him in the position to "give back."

As Spanky began calling for one-million one hundred thousand, Ressler started shouting: "Sell the car! Sell the car!" Soon those around him were echoing the chant.

Jackson called Ressler to the stage, and began the countdown to the sale. As Jackson cried "Third and last call," he handed the gavel to Leno and told him to hammer it sold. The entire transaction took less than 2 minutes and 30 seconds. Applause erupted and television and still cameras closed around the buyer and the M.C.

"You could say I was inspired because of my dad who was a car salesman for twenty-five years," Ressler replied to the first of hundreds of questions. "I've got a passion for what I do and for how I got here," he explained in a more recent interview. "We did everything Chevy in our family. My dad worked all the time and I really didn't want to go into that business. But it was in my blood and it still is."

Ressler took delivery of the car at the Bowling Green assembly plant on July 22, 2008. His 2009 ZR1 #5900001, the subject of this chapter, joined his extensive collection of Corvettes that also includes 1953 number 003, the oldest of the legends in this book.

The car is about performance, *0 to 60 miles an hour in 3.3 seconds. The standing-start quarter-mile required 11.4 seconds, and the car hit 125.5 miles per hour. Chevrolet reported its top speed at 205 miles per hour.*

INDEX

The best part of doing any new book is meeting the people who step forward to offer information, help, vehicles to photograph, and other assistance. We were particularly fortunate with this project and so we wish to recognize and thank:

Kevin and Kathy Adams, Rochester, IN; John and Cathy Amgwert, Bullhead City, AZ; Hal Barwood, Portland, OR; Ed Baumgarten, Director of Photography, Mid America Motorworks, Effingham, IL; Jeffrey Belskus, President, Indianapolis Motor Speedway, Indianapolis, IN; Ellen Bireley, Director, Indianapolis Motor Speedway Hall of Fame Museum, Indianapolis, IN; Peter Blackford, Business Manager, CH Motorcars LLC, Naples, FL; Peter and Gayle Brock, Redmond, WA; Reeves Callaway, Callaway Cars, Laguna Beach, CA; John Carefoot, Cincinnati, OH; Chris Chessnoe, Callaway Cars, Old Lyme, CT; Amy Christie, RM Auctions, Blenheim, Ontario, Canada; Miles Collier, CH Motorcars LLC, Naples, FL; Paul Deutschman, Deutschman Design, Montreal, Quebec, Canada; Dan Edwards, Manager of Track Racing Operations, Indianapolis Motor Speedway, Indianapolis, IN; Wayne Ellwood, co-founder, www.RegistryofCorvetteRaceCars.com; Franz Estereicher, Rochester Hills, MI; John Fitch, Lime Rock, CT; Scott George, President, CH Motorcars LLC, Naples, FL; Jim Gessner, Mentone, CA, co-founder www.RegistryofCorvetteRaceCars.com; Robin Gibson, Indian Hills, OH; Steve Goldin, Homestead, FL; Rodney Green, General Motors Heritage Collection, Warren, MI; Dick Guldstrand, Burbank, CA; Natalia Hipp, Barrett-Jackson Auction Company, Scottsdale, AZ; Dan and Rea Hoetker, Cincinnati, OH; Gib Hufstader, Utica, MI; Jan Hyde, co-founder, www.RegistryofCorvetteRaceCars.com; Jim Jaeger, Indian Hills, OH; Delmo Johnson, Addison, TX; Janice Kinder, Mid-America Motorworks, Effingham, IL; Richard Korkes, Korky's Kustom Kars, Palm Springs, CA; Gary Kuck, Lincoln, NE; Tony Lapine, stylist/designer General Motors Studio X, Baden-Baden, Germany; Fred Larimer, Orange, CA; Patrick Lemay, Carlisle Events, Carlisle, PA; Phil Leonhard, CH Motorcars, Naples, FL; Kevin Mackay, Corvette Repair, Inc., Valley Stream, NY; Dave McLellan, chief engineer Corvette, retired, Holly, MI; Ron McQueeney, Director of Photography, Indianapolis Motor Speedway, Indianapolis, IN; Vince and Nancy Mercuri, Carmel, IN; Judy Miller, Miller Family Collection, Carlisle, PA; Lance Miller, Senior Manager, Carlisle Events, Carlisle, PA; Joe Miner, Newport Beach, CA; Mike Mueller, Kennesaw, GA; Mike Nardo, Red Lion, PA; Richard Newton, automotive historian, Naples, FL; Dave Ressler, Bozeman, MT; D. Randy Riggs, Novato, CA; Matthew Robbins, Inverness, CA; Tony Ruddick, Scottsdale, AZ; Dr. Dick and Eve Thompson, Wellington, FL; Mike and Laurie Yager, and Blake Yager, Mid-America Motorworks, Effingham, IL; Harry Yeaggy, Cincinnati, OH; Dan Wendt, Oxford, OH; and Lori Worman, Mid-America Motorworks, Effingham, IL.

Last, but most of all, thanks to my friend Dave Wendt for producing the amazing photographs that illustrate this book. Dave's lighting technique and his imagination brought these cars out of history and into a true form of automotive sculpture and art.